PSYCHE HISTORIES:
• PRESIDENCIES • FIRST LADIES

PSYCHE HISTORIES:
• PRESIDENCIES • FIRST LADIES

GERALD MIDDENTS

PSYCHE HISTORIES: • PRESIDENCIES • FIRST LADIES

iUniverse books may be ordered through booksellers or by contacting:

iUniverse
1663 Liberty Drive
Bloomington, IN 47403
www.iuniverse.com
844-349-9409

ISBN: 978-1-6632-2094-3 (sc)
ISBN: 978-1-6632-2095-0 (e)

Print information available on the last page.

iUniverse rev. date: 04/13/2021

CONTENTS

PREFACE: PRESDIENTIAL SHADOWS ARE SHOWING

With the installation of the 46th President;

Citizens may see our history unfolding.

This will be is a unique experience

As many observe this occasion.

Americans engage in a new stage;

Future citizens will evaluate this age.

President Biden has had his inauguration;

In 2017, President Trump had his occasion.

This is turning point in history;

We look ahead with fantasy.

We also review our own past;

In contributing to what will be!

As this book gives attention to both;

For deciding the Presidential oath.

As America is among global leaders,

This message is designed for readers!

Assess candidates on "policy decision-making!"

How will they lead other into collaborating!

Humanities future will also be at stake;

So our decision is a key one to make!

DISCOVERING UNCONSCIOUS SHADOWS

Is your own Shadow showing?

Do you know what it is revealing?

It is different from your persona;

It may not know about America.

Since human Shadows are unconscious

Persons may become somewhat oblivious.

Psychological processes are necessary

For it to become disclosed publicly!

Awareness of personal Shadows is a key;

To be balancing the roles of publicity.

Persons may have little understanding

How to manage this as bewildering.

Personal histories of known public officials

May initially open our mind as individuals.

By reflecting, we understand ourselves better;

This book can become helpful to you as reader.

.

When all declare their candidacy and all their announcements are made,

Their presidential faces become common parlance through all of media.

What their public face shows is primarily one component of personality,

Not apparent are their real self and dark side that is much more shadowy.

This marketing image is tailored as a "surface layer" of their public front,

But their Shadow components are hidden by their unconscious from us.

Personas are actor's face not of themselves but of a fictional character,

Persona is a mask that is worn to portray the real persona by an actor.

Our revered leaders are known to have made lasting key contributions,

Presidents are valued for solving problems with their ingenious solutions.

Those who leave the countries better off are those who are remembered,

Posterity deserves the best leaders who tackle conflicts so they are solved.

There are huge international challenges awaiting better solutions soon,

Domestic issues are chronic in America and economically much of Europe.

We become preoccupied with legislations about gay and lesbian marriages,

"Don't Ask, Don't Tell" contemporarily condenses many hidden agendas.

CHAPTER 1: NOTED EARLY PRESIDENTS OF THIS NATION

History remembers George Washington as a General and first President,

Yes, he not only was a military leader but also a leader who was moderate.

Without his strategic leadership, the Revolutionary War may have been lost,

He showed balanced vision that inspired others to contribute to the cause.

This first President also benefited from his very helpful wife, Martha!

She was the Mother of several children at Mount Vernon at home!

While the General was fighting wars, Martha kept home without him!

Then when he became the first President, she lived in Washington!

History also recognizes Abraham Lincoln for emancipating the slaves,

Yes, many are awe-struck with the horrendous Civil War and casualties,

A few recall that Lincoln also laid the foundation for opening the West,

He laid groundwork for establishing the trans-continental railroads.

Mrs. Lincoln, his wife, also possessed skills to be extremely adaptable;

While first living in Illinois, where her husband was their Governor!

Then she raised their children while Abraham was extremely busy;

In the 1860's, when he was the President, she was the First Lady!

During the Gilded Age, financial empire expanded into corporations;

David Rockefeller became very wealthy man with his own railroads.

Other wealthy corporations then had very little accountability;

By 1911, government broke up these very large monopolies.[1]

Understandably wars receive undue attention with even more fascinations,

But domestic developments are less dramatic but offer enormous solutions.

Theodore Roosevelt was a noted Colonel in the Spanish-American War,

His enduring legacies are National Parks with monuments at Black Hills.

Woodrow Wilson was a Princeton President who supported U.S. isolation,

Entering World War I's last years; Then establish the League of Nations.

The Peace of Versailles had ominous consequences leading into WW II,

Wilson's idealism laid predicates for subsequently the United Nations.

---

[1] Zubook, Shoshana, January 31, 2021, "The Knowledge Coup," <u>The New York Times.</u>

In 1912 and 1916 when Wilson was elected, women were not able to vote!

They were not permitted to vote for the Presidents until into the 1920's.

Efforts by women had been made since the middle of the 19th century;

The United States was slow in permitting women to vote in this country!

Mrs. Wilson was the First Lady in Washington during World War I;

Then later her husband, Woodrow, would then become unusually ill.

Mrs. Wilson had a challenging role as the President's interpreter.

This became a puzzling role while President Wilson became even sicker!

In a recent _Foreign Affairs_[2] an article "The End of Wilsonian Era,"

Reviewed the mysterious illness of President Woodrow Wilson.

Mead claimed this was "the death of liberal internationalism!"

Eliot A. Cohen claimed that Wilson also ignored the pandemic then.

Between these two World Wars major developments were very sparse,

Europe became a continental disaster with bad negative importance.

Greed in the stock markets in America led onward to financial crisis,

The "Great Depression" became an abomination that was disastrous.

---

[2] Mead, W.R., "The End of Wilsonian Era,"

There are untold stories about how each President did not ask nor tell,

The Presidency has such enormous responsibility citizens cannot quell.

Managing these "Top Secrets" is problematic in our current democracies,

Open transparency becomes a major challenge just short of hypocrisies.

VOLATILE 1930'S THROUGH 1950'S

Early during 1930's Great Depression, then World War II and Cold War,

This nation was threatened to its core so arose "The Greatest Generation!"

Such powerful forces can also stimulate opposite reactions in due time,

As assassinations, riots, strong-arm tactics and even religious change!

I personally remember impacts of this Great Depression in the thirties,

Born in 1933, we had enough to eat by living on a farm with my family.

My Republican Father confided only one time he once voted for a Democrat,

He voted for Franklin Delano Roosevelt, not for Hoover from our "Io-way!"

President Roosevelt had major wars to confront and a Great Depression,

He faced them with all of his energy while investing all of his attention!

But like Moses, he did not get to see the ending of wars, dying historically,

Winning victory of two wars and launching of the United Nations globally.

President Roosevelt was an exuberantly bouncy exterior in his persona,

He compensated for very crippling polio by compensating in the public.

The 1940's America was intensely focused on defeating Japan and Germany,

President Roosevelt wore out after 13 years of such grueling challenges.

The President's wife, Eleanor, developed remarkable skills in speaking;

She managed their home and children so he could continue leading!

Then later she was recognized as the Founder of the United Nations!

Eleanor Roosevelt was also phenomenal as a leading global women!

Delano died in office just before these two wars ended as the Allies succeeded,

He had seen the whole Free World through two devastating war theaters,

His leadership is noted for both victories in was and also for his New Deal.

I heard this radio news on our farm rushing out to tell my seasoned Dad!

Only a seventh grader, I did not know how to place this in perspective,

My brother was flying B-29 missions over Japan all that very spring.

We worried about Mel who was ten years older and was my own hero,

Vice-President Truman was thrust into decisions that had to be made.

Harry Truman was among the few transparent public officials to serve,

As Vice-President who was a candid Missourian he was rarely artificial.

He faced Stalin and Churchill in testy negotiations for the United Nations,

His decisions ended the Japanese War with devastating atomic weapons.

Secretly, Vice-President Truman was not aware of the Manhattan Project.

It was so highly classified so that Congress did not know about this subject.

Typical of this secrecy was the strategy that participants did not know,

Each had a small piece, but only a very limited group was entrusted!

The world was depleted with so much devastation that was extensive,

Compassion was elicited among many people who could be pensive.

The Marshall Plan created an atmosphere of forgiveness and renewal,

Bombed-out Europe was reconstructed; Japan became democratic political.

Roosevelt's genius pragmatism led to fruition in America economically,

He had forged this industrial platform in our industrial manufacturing.

The immense indebtedness incurred in order to win two terrible wars,

Was mostly converted into rebuilding civilian progress with rewards

A monumental set of pillars was introducing the GI Bill for education!

Many war veterans were financially encouraged to enroll in school.

Those who had never dreamed of college education studied for degrees,

Many whose education had been interrupted returned very thankfully.

The GI Bill jump enabled those young citizens who have served nobly,

Survivors remember the trauma of dying comrades ending bravely.

They became "The Great Generation" who rejuvenated this country,

In their memory, America forged ahead to lead our nation globally.

In one hundred sixty years, this nation led the world onward into peace,

The rivalry between communism and democracy threateningly hostile.

The "Cold War" was kept cool so that hot battles did not lead to a test,

The "Soviet Union" and its Eastern nations challenged Allies in the West.

My freshman year at Iowa University my assigned topic to defend Truman,

He had boldly fired General McArthur who proposed invading China.

In this research about his Presidential decision, I supported the President,

His uncanny capacity to balance very tough decisions was very evident!

The Korean "Police Action" started but quickly became a full-fledged war,

Truman had to face down General MacArthur to not use atomic bombs!

Truman's place in history has continued to rise as one who could decide,

Not a complicated man, what you saw is what America got without pride!

Harry Truman was among the rare transparent elected public officials,

He served humbly as Vice-President quickly confronting internationals.

In Truman, "what you see is what you get" consistent with "show me!"

His candid Missouri genuineness was fresh air without any pretending.

The Korean War was an early struggle between rivals through surrogates,

Those of us who served in military service know about nuclear threats,

So much economic profit was made in the military-industrial complex,

While the American economy prospered, dangerous weapons benefit.

My service in the U.S. Air Force as a Top-Secret Officer for nuclear testing,

I was entrusted with administratively managing Top Secret handling.

At the base as Assistant Adjutant cleared to Atomic Energy Commission,

We only had pieces of the bigger picture in doing this ominous mission.

President Eisenhower warned of weapons for-profit very perceptively,

   He also gave an impetus to the building of transcontinental highways!

Ironically this road system was designed to move military equipment,

   Predominantly this transportation system was a domestic investment.

General Dwight Eisenhower served his country as a dedicated soldier,

   His masterful role as Field General in Europe was very incredible.

He dealt with enormous military egos from England and France,

   He was trusted by military and nations that were major advances.

As a Veteran serving in Air Force in the 1950's, we had confidence in him;

   Major advances in nuclear weapons by both America and Russians.

The American economy ribbed up to become a powerful machine!

   Stability and economic prosperity helped to settle the Japanese!

"Ike" possessed a friendly smile that lubricated his military toughness,

   Occasionally he was manipulated while his flexibility was a real asset.

His persona was consistent in both military and civilian responsibilities,

   He was perceptive about people and also about the expenses of armies.

His conclusion has not been taken seriously enough in budgetary account,

He advised the world about the dangers of military-industrial complex.

Yes, he had weaknesses that he made efforts to seek sound counsel,

His Secretary of State was pre-occupied with "The Domino Theory."

This dubious doctrine of "communist containment" became a disaster,

Contrary to military science doctrine of 1950's was very appropriate.

America should not become involved in another land war in Asia,

Civilian leadership failed us by engaging in Viet Nam as "advisors!"

Another impetus arose as Russia launched its' space missile "Sputnik!"

America's response led Kennedy to motivate our NASA space projects.

Along with the earlier National Defense Acts pioneered in Ike's term,

America launched not only space travel to the moon but partnerships.

Expansive 1960's and 1970's

Television media and technological communications draw actors,

Very find genuine people are consistent with their face to voters!

John and Jackie Kennedy conveyed the artificial aura of "Camelot!"

Together this couple created simulated illusions that were global.

Attractive people grab audiences that are surprisingly just superficial,

With coaching, lighting and media prompting they appear special!

Contemporary audiences are very visually oriented to watch images,

These can be rapidly spliced together to make these the big stories.

Even young Rupert Murdock was escorted about the White House,

John F. personally showed this young Australian round and about.

Kennedy even shared hot information with this 30 year-old Rupert,

A Presidential Aide had Rupert detained when leaving New York.

Both of these heirs were descendents of very well healed families,

Both were in the lime light of their respective native counties.

The diplomatic finesse of Kennedy was in a more refined taste,

Murdock did not imitate his Father but made stops in haste.

Kennedy's assassination led to very mixed blessings of contradiction!

I clearly remember that we were eating lunch at our family table.

Walter Cronkite solemnly announced: "The President is Dead!"

We were stunned as was the world about what happened in Dallas.

With the mourners in the U.S., Kennedy's wife, then faced bravely,

   She effectively helped Americans to handle immediate grieving.

Many people in the world were supportive and understanding;

   Huge decisions followed that Americans to keep continuing!

Friday noon to Sunday morning, I changed my sermon for Sunday,

   My message to connect us to the historic faithfulness of human folly,

My congregation was shook to their core, but steadiness was in order,

   They knew that my patriotic steadfastness helped them as comforter.

As citizens we discovered the Constitutional plan for succession,

   Vice President Lyndon Johnson was sworn in quickly as President!

Yes, Americans and the world were deeply shook in these crisis,

   But our Constitution had vision to provide guiding this transition.

Responses of Americans healed after shock moving as a crucible,

   Johnson pioneered civil rights and also health care for susceptible.

His vision hoped for both "Guns and Butter" in his "Great Society!"

   But butter moved the economy while guns led to more acrimony.

The 1960's and 1970's were notoriously superficial as television emerged,

Traditional constraints were shattered so also just boundaries splurged.

Fluidity relaxing restraints with "freedom," "civil rights" and "free love,"

Were also pushed to limits as old practices were out of here and shove!

Lyndon Johnson was an enormously energetic legislator in the Senate,

He was rushed into Presidential office quickly with Kennedy's death.

He managed legislative agendas thru with prodding and intimidation,

He was a Senator where his ideal goal moved much quick legislation.

These Presidents seemed to be "larger-than-life" in their leadership,

The 1950-60's ushered in the expression of America's partnership.

The Eastern Soviet Bloc threatened as a dangerous nuclear power,

Equally powerful West held MAD (Mutually Assured Destruction).

Johnson images tarnished when he tried to hide his agenda in war,

His management of Vietnam War was very soon no longer valid!

Seeing that his social and military goals were impossible to achieve,

He "will not seek and would not seek" to run for a second full term.

"Lady Byrd" Johnson was Linden's long-time wife from Texas;

   She maintained poise throughout his long-time political leader!

As she rose to the challenge of becoming the nation's First Lady;

   Responsible for rearing a daughter was another challenge.

Power was a contaminating factor in Johnson's effectiveness and demise,

   He desperately expended for both "Guns and Butter" as no surprise.

But his manipulative style crept deeply into his Persona and Shadow,

   He responded both ambitiously and with vanity that was also inside.

Nixon could be effective in diplomacy with the Chinese and Russians,

   But in the 1972 election, my mate detected Nixon was inconsistent.

He did not communicate genuine consistency so was even defective,

   She detected his duplicity much quicker than many older executives.

Richard Nixon known as "Tricky Dick" waited for twenty-two years,

   Eight years as Vice-President, then as President winning the vote later.

His shadowy side remained hidden from even his own intimate family,

   His intentional deceptions uncovered facing impeachment bravely.

Nixon's own secrecy fostered early themes of "Don't Ask, Don't Tell!"

Like Johnson before, vital information from the public was withheld.

American's confidence in central government was almost beyond repair,

The Constitution held firmly when a very orderly transfer of power.

Nixon was then an impeached disaster, who broke through with China;

United States did not have essential leadership in the next three years,

America awaits leadership comprehending both themselves and citizens,

Wars, recessions, bubbles, de-regulations, deception are shenanigans.

Mrs. Nixon maintained her calm poise throughout his Presidency;

The Mother of two daughters gave her major responsibilities!

When her husband resigned, she managed major adjustments!

Her dignity was remarkably calm throughout these challenges.

Gerald Ford, an uncomplicated leader of the House of Representatives,

His image as a Michigan football hero appealed while not legislative.

His contender, Jimmie Carter, was a Navy officer and peanut farmer,

Carter's genuineness attracted voters who tired of him as governor.

While Carter had been a very honorable Governor of Georgia before,

Washington dynamism was almost bewildering to his peanut store.

He brought inexperienced cabinet members untested in Washington,

His personal life has been impeccable but naïve on big shenanigans.

The fatal attempt to rescue hostages from Tehran was very high risk,

When this mission failed, Carter's Presidency took a very large dip.

He also did not address the pending issues of "Don't Ask! Don't Tell,"

This issue was also kicked down the road paved all the way to hell.

President Carter's wife has been a very serene helpmate for Jimmy!

She dealt with both television coverage and travel internationally!

Their three children were poised including their teenage daughter;

She contributed her composure when her husband faced danger!

CHAPTER 2: TURNING POINT: 1980'S

America has had a football star, a peanut farmer and Hollywood actor,

Plus an inept privileged dynasty, a virile wonk without a benefactor.

When will we have a President who can function from the center?

The polarized ideologists whip citizens by extremities and banter.

Military in Lebanon, Central America, Grenada, Iraq and Afghanistan,

Have been unintelligent adventures that do not merit trusting America.

America has been in limbo from 1977-2008 vacillating unfortunately,

Leadership has become increasingly partisan without balancing polarity.

Illustrations of personas flesh out these manipulative marketing images,

Versatile actresses and actors created the role by taking on a staged display.

Ronald Reagan as an actor had talent to take on different stage personas,

He portrayed cowboys, sports announcers, advertising and "The Gipper!"

What voters viewed was merely Reagan's trained public performances,

He adopted his image to diverse roles to who were very different places.

He could convey toughness that was skin deep or superficial religiosity,

When he was expected to be a global leader, he portrayed it pompously.

Reagan exuded a confidence publicly he could not back up with insights,

He did not ask penetrating questions so he received primarily "sights."

His incapacity to process negative data showed his denial and diversions,

He only wanted to receive good news insulating his optimistic visions.

He also perpetuated the false images of America's "Exceptionalism,"

Reagan tuned out America's vulnerabilities by looking Presidential.

His untested optimism failed to see the hidden ditches of capitalism,

He instead focused his attention on challenging Soviet Communism.

Reagan's personal needs to be optimistic and so positive were limits,

One can distort his effectiveness by identifying only his few benefits.

He was blindsided to the crass greed and selfishness of capitalists,

As his legacy is more about "Not Asking Limits, Just Talking a Lot!"

Rupert Murdoch admired Reagan's style in his "Unified Field Theory,"

Both loved the free market like Libertarians flaunting the regulatory.

Both were anti-labor trying to be "Alpha Males" with political power,

They loved grandiosity as deal makers both with multi-marriages.

Rupert was a newspaperman who promoted tabloids everywhere,

They valued "functionalism" so that they could be "untrumpable!"

Unreflective showmen, they grabbed the platform before the public,

Both initially were more liberal, but middle-age turned conservative.

They had comfort with conflicts as they could see this was newsworthy,

They themselves were not in military service, others served heroically.

Both Reagan and Rupert tried creating impressions of power leverage,

Sometimes they bluffed their way into newsy positions very politically.

Their similar positions in economics and politics created the eighties,

They did not sufficient perspectives to evaluate their later heritage.

Rupert was a sinister bargainer in big deals in American and Britain
/
Both liked Margaret Thatcher valuing her tough public demeanor.

George "H.W. Bush" was a contrast with Ronald Reagan as running mate,

He swallowed Reagan' s "supply-side economics" after criticizing it late.

He possessed a global menu as a veteran but also was had a blind spot,

His "wimpiness" also embarrassed his older son serving as President.

Murdock had a distinct distaste for George H.W. Bush from the start,

Their styles and personalities were not at all similar but very different.

Murdock's television stations and newspapers covered the Gulf War,

But with-drawing from Iraq was not a Murdock strategy from afar.

Eight years as Vice-President, then "H.W." engaged in the Gulf War,

But he was blind to the economic disasters that were upon all of us.

Elder Bush failed to address the downtown in the American economy,

He did not ask penetrating questions that will occur in democracy.

The so-called Bush dynasty remains to be an undefined phenomenon,

Yes, there are several generations of this elite family for the curious.

World affairs have both benefited but also destructively damaged,

The outcomes into the future are only now being fully evaluated.

Mrs. Bush was composed during her husband's term as President!

She had a large family to rear and her role was Mother was evident!

She provided balance for George H.W. during his role as a leader;

Including the careful Mothering for their son who is George W.

Clinton was unique in his diverse public images in 1992 did appear,

His wonky policy verbosity sounds so good, but is he also surreal?

Hillary also projected aggression that may threaten Bill's manhood?

As Secretary of State, she was supported by their global neighborhood!

Clinton could talk very positively for public appearances as uncanny,

But his major health care proposals were then not moved forward.

Approaches of secret planning were an error to keep public informed,

As this major domestic effort his first two years made him forlorn.

In his next moves, his was naïveté with the military became apparent,

He advocated "Don't' Ask; Don't Tell" now as a military instrument.

Hiding only perpetuated the tortuous road of both lesbians and gays,

This policy neither solved this challenge nor gave it clear guidance.

Hillary, his wife, demonstrated real balance as Bill Clinton's spouse;

Her talents became evident during his Presidency and as Senator!

Very rarely, has this nation had such remarkable dual leadership!

Her composure continues to be evident domestically and globally!

He did learn in hindsight that he was vulnerable to sexual power,

His managing "self" was unable to moderate his persona and shadow.

Bill remains a mysterious person who migrated from poverty to riches,

In retrospect, he likely would revise how he might react to his wishes.

While he matured in the Office of President, he had gaps in wisdom,

His high energy and spirited campaigning made him very winsome.

But he failed to recognize both human and personal vulnerabilities,

That unregulated free markets can create bubbles but also hostilities.

Rupert Murdock was ambivalent about Bill as President and Hillary,

Yes, Rupert zeroed his reporters on the affair of Bill with Lewinsky.

This type of tabloid news was Rupert's favorite type of broad coverage,

Hot stories sold newspapers while he also made profit with TV media.

Murdock has mixed impressions of Hillary as a presidential candidate,

He has difficulties relating to powerful women like Secretary of State.

His own Mother was a dominating woman whom he later resented,

Rupert's three marriages with additional children became represented.

AMERICA'S SHADOW

The United States claimed to have real interests in the Middle East;

    These global involvements also possessed inherent consequences!

The Middle East and the Northeast of Africa are very complicated;

    So many expected significant outcomes typically have occurred.

With the revolution in Egypt opening up possibilities for democracy

    This stimulated reflections on how to overcome these autocracies!

America's Founding Fathers and French advanced liberty and freedoms

    These Enlightenment values held key meaning in liberated kingdoms!

The young and old of Egypt had been suppressed for many decades;

    Observing how Western cultures flourished but not in the oldest.

Surprisingly, the young Egyptians displaying considerable restraint,

    Their notable disciplined actions are rarely found among the faint!

Perceptive writers in America repeatedly tried to assess our status;

    They looked critically into what is called "America's Apparatus."

The Egyptian rebellion gave pause for all the Middle East nations;

    As courageous young Egyptians generated their demonstrations!

They saw the lack of opportunity for their talents and ambitions;

They tried many efforts to appeal to Mubarak with partitions.

Unemployment and depression limited their real opportunities;

This incited many to reach the tipping point for responsibilities.

They grabbed the "Horns of Freedom" by wrestling old leaders!

Mubarak was entrenched with the Army and the wealthier.

After 50 years of the "State of Emergency" and domination

They took the initiative stimulated by success in Tunisia!

This younger generation saw their actions were very timely;

Act now! Or they would regret an inheritance for family.

This window of opportunity was in 2011 for their action;

They put their lives on the line to take to act for rebellion.

TIMELY REFLECTIONS

As the oldest democracy that experimented to be successful;

Americans may be able to help Egypt to find fulfillment.

Constitutional criteria help pursue freedom and equality;

Could America help the Egyptians discover new civility?

How do global people evaluate America's contributions?

The world today has wide ranges of democratic opinions.

Respect for America teeters from doubts to sheer adulation;

This may be disconcerting about global unease of opinions.

The world today wonders about whether to emulate democracy;

Is the American experiment actually adaptable to their ways?

We may not be fully aware of the variety of global perceptions;

American policies may not fit them after we make reflections.

While teaching in India, I was asked to share my reflections;

The Indian comment indicated negative view of America.

He stated: "We do not like everything your government does!"

My response: "Do you like all that the Indian government does?"

This respected Indian citizen admitted he had some negative views;

He did not like many of India's government current practices!

This candid exchange was both important and also expected

Our personal perceptions helped to discover mutual respect!

DYNASTIES OF THE BUSH AND MURDOCH

What Bush represents is accented by the people he hired,

One is Cheney who was a strange Administrator who fires.

In 2000, he was President of Haliburton, Inc. in Dallas,

He was appointed by Bush as V-P thinking he was cool.

Cheney was first appointed by George H.W. in his cabinet,

Soon he became a big confidant of Bush as his negotiator.

What does this illustrate about the Bush interest himself?

Was he interested in corporate power or in his own power?

Check the professional record of Bush in order for you to see,

He was portending to be a tough Republican who does not agree.

Did he sell out to big money interest so he made money?

What about the education of George H.W. Bush about security?

Bush saw himself as a powerful business operator corporately,

Cheney had been deceptively recruited blindly to his vulnerability.

As expected, Bush and Cheney denied these accusations publicly,

They were both crafty at manipulation without public responsibility.

Cheney had given the overt image of a conservative Republican,

    Answer this question: What now is an educated public servant?

Since he has been with Haliburton, Inc. his backspins had left,

    Was he in the grips of self-greed or was he ready to become bereft?

Check both Bush and Cheney in their performance historically,

    They were trying to save their hid or to sound so complacently?

Had Cheney been manipulated by an experienced entrepreneur?

    Was he being recruited as a V.P. or a very crafty manipulator?

Were Bush and Cheney's allegiance being put on a clear line?

    Were they primarily for themselves, or were they able to sublime?

Sublimation of their aggressive nature was clearly transparent,

    As they disguised their self-interest above America's children?

When have corporate financiers placed children above self?

    What evidence is there that corporations help anyone else?

Who is able to testify on their behalf that has any credibility?

    Why do they repeatedly seek power with social responsibly?

This poem is posing questions that the public needs to know,

   These powerful hungry wealthy needed to confront a public show.

Whose interest was primary and whose future was being ignored?

   Did they have public responsibility or were they just carnivores?

Cheney showed meager evidence to be allied with education,

   Have the nation's Schools shown any evidence of progression?

The legal-business model of addressing educational issues,

   Failed miserably while all of America slipped internationally.

CHAPTER 3: THE BUSH-CHENEY BLINDSIDE

Everyone has a blind spot in their own eyes that is apparent,

   This blind spot is located where optical nerves enter retina.

If you do not know this now, in time you may simply discover it,

   As we do not notice this blind spot when we cover this blank.

George was primarily focused on the big financial transactions,

   His biographers note that he focused on business negotiations.

Consequently, he was unaware of his blind spots in public policy,

   But his V.P Cheney was very aware of how to exploit it publicly.

Combining Cheney's business acumen and "w's" simplicity,

   They may have created a blend of both strengths naturally.

If they did not have insight into the blind spot of each other,

   They entered a mysterious reality that they could manuever.

Bush's wealth and preoccupation with corporate enterprises,

   Partially blended with the technology of Cheney's blindsides.

The investigations that proceeded in America were then found,

   Just where this President and V.P. did not know they were blind.

Their own Administration's record has been researched publicly,

    Uncovered their denial of awareness that may have been duplicity.

Together, Cheney and Bush had their four eyes for perceptions,

    They did not combine their strengths to cover their obsessions.

When powerful people and their legal counsels are unaware,

    The physiological blindness is metaphorically as vulnerable.

The primary strength of each one is only a small coverage,

    Their blind spots may be complicating their own umbrage.

Neither Bush nor Cheney were balanced on how teams work?

    They focused on their goals, but did they notice their own quirks?

Powerful persons have blind spots that make them vulnerable

    To their own Shadows that propel them ahead but not humble.

Shadows are often unconscious to people obsessed with power,

    They operate on their public personas for the public observer.

When powerful are not aware of how to control their Shadow,

    They are subject to very distorted images of their own power.

The biographies of the Bush family reveal little reflection,

They apparently were pre-occupied with their own obsessions.

With floods of public media coverage, they were susceptible,

To imagining their own imperviousness to be all-powerful.

Historically, powerful people have been subject to downfalls,

Because their human vanity blinded them to these pitfalls.

Numerous historical accounts reveal powerful who then fail,

Often because they start to believe their own glory will trail.

Human quests for power are very tempting to those wealthy,

Their accouterments bolster their own images as powerfully.

Take this analysis as a tentative hypothesis for their downfall,

At their zenith of public notoriety, they were more vulnerable.

Al Gore s complicated personality, was intellectually superior to Bush,

Both privileged at Harvard; Both unable to do what they should.

"w's" compensatory defenses were both sooner or later bound to show,[3]

By trying frantically to be a "Decisive War President" did not flow.

---

[3]   One of his Professors personally shared 'w's limits with this author.

31

Dick Cheney's persona was selected to cover "w's" known weaknesses,

Character defects were revealing both did have serious limitations.

Together "Bush-Cheney" did not possess global gravitas or perspectives,

They stumbled into similar errors of judgment plus in their decisions.

This strange "team" of leaders with a powerful VP acted imposingly,

Their narrow experiences and education were evident very quickly.

Apparently "being the deciders" fascinated them with big leadership,

But they failed to ask penetrating questions to stay in their blindness.

When Presidents have a propensity to act without data so decisively,

The whole nation and the world suffer from their lack of curiosity.

"w" failed to convince the world that he could lead the United States,

His decisions lost America's trust with a significant lack of respect!

America and humanity were suffering Bush-Cheney presumptuousness,

They never possessed the ingredients expected for America's Presidents.

Jointly their leadership domestically and globally has been disastrous,

Millions suffered bad consequences while they may never recover.

They also did not provide key leadership in managing this economy,

Their juvenile ideas of human goodness saw rules as unnecessary.

Leaving two terrible wars to be managed more effectively and justly,

They also abandoned the American economy to Wall Street greedy!

Was this team of President and V-P too fascinated with entitlements?

Assuming that their records would carry them into the history books?

Already historians have had difficulty identifying lasting achievements,

Their heritage as leaders has been compounded by doubtful significance.

"w" assumed himself wanting to be a hero as "Educational President,"

"w's" dubious debut may have become his own compensatory event.

His scholarly record at Yale, University of North Texas and Harvard,

Left ample room in his noggin that had never registered as "FULL!"

His attempts in Texas were a very mixed record of educational success,

Using a business management model, he left Texas in a very big mess!

His apparent fixation on "tests" registered as he was not good at studies,

They were so proud of "No Child Left Behind" like playground duties.

A ten-year experiment with all children of America results came out!

Entitled: <u>The Death and the Life of the Great American School System!</u>[4]

"w's" was nominated for riding herd on national school kids who rebelled,

She left in disgust in negative program evaluation that never excelled!

Moreover, deadly outcomes were shown in the negative toll upon teachers,

Their effectiveness in educating students with half quitting in five years.

This failing outcome has already hampering America's world leadership,

Creativity and innovation took a dive instead of having statesmanship.

So what has resulted from "w's" experiment for our school children?

Evidence reports America had then slipped behind over ten nations.

Likewise, the school children have suffered in Iraq and Afghanistan,

Iraq's respectable education system in the last century does not stand.

In Afghanistan Greg Mortenson was a superior educator than our military,

His book <u>Stones into Schools</u>[5] has provided education for young girls,

Military leaders were required to learn his approach to Tribal Leaders,

The war had annihilated Afghan schools, Mortenson was seen as restorer.

---

[4] RaVilch, Diane.

[5] Mortenson

So what might be concluded about the impact of "w" on our education?

Was he an amateur who rose in government power to make decisions?

Empirical data were revealing the decline of achievement even on our tests,

We were being left with a generation of students who are behind the rest!

Bush-Cheney left another negative imprint on this nation's reputation:

Their inability to work toward common ground fostering polarization.

Washington had major problems in functioning with some collaboration,

Disparities between rich and poor were a huge economic manifestation.

With enormous national debt incurred with war and lax tax policies,

Any successor to Bush-Cheney was bound to have major difficulties.

When predecessors leave baggage that was carried into the next term,

The problems created over decades cannot be solved by more years.

When prior leadership leaves the next President with two wars to fight,

Along with a devastating economic recession so nothing looks bright.

The twenty-first century had experienced excesses of selfish greed,

America was polarized into rebellious factions with nothing agreed.

DYNASTIES OF BUSH AND MURDOCH

What Bush represented was accented by the people he hired,

One was Cheney who was a strange Administrator who fires.

In 2000, he was the President of Haliburton, Inc. in Dallas,

He was appointed by Bush as V-P thinking he was cool.

Cheney was first appointed by George H.W. in his cabinet,

Soon he became a big confidant of Bush as his negotiator.

What did this illustrate about the Bush's interest himself?

Was he interested in corporate power or in his own power?

Check the professional record of Dick in order for you to see,

He was portending to be a tough Republican who did not agree.

Did he sell out to big money interests so he made money?

What about the education of George and Bush for security?

Bush saw himself as a powerful business operator corporately,

Cheney had been deceptively recruited blind to his vulnerability.

Expect that Bush and Cheney to denied these accusations publicly,

They were both crafty at manipulation without public responsibility.

Cheney had given the overt image of a conservative Republican,

Answer this question: What now is an educated public servant?

Since he had been with Haliburton, Inc. his backspins have left,

Was he in the grips of self-greed or is he ready to become bereft?

Check both Bush and Cheney in their performance historically,

Were they trying to save their hid or to sound so complacently?

Had Cheney been manipulated by an experienced entrepreneur?

Was he being recruited as a V.P. or a very crafty manipulator?

Were Bush and Cheney's allegiance being put on a clear line?

Were they primarily for themselves, or were they able to sublime?

Sublimation of their aggressive nature was clearly transparent,

Were they disguising their self-interest above America's children?

When have corporate financiers placed children above self?

What evidence was there that corporations help anyone else?

Who was able to testify on their behalf that had any credibility?

Why did they repeatedly seek power with social responsibly?

This poem is posing questions that the public needs to know,

These power hungry wealthy need to confront a public show.

Whose interest was primary and whose future was being ignored?

Did they have public responsibility or were they just omnivores?

Cheney showed meager evidence to be allied with education,

Did the nation's Schools show any evidence of progression?

The legal-business model of addressing educational issues

Failed miserably while all of America slipped internationally.

Senator Howard Baker posed questions to investigate Watergate:
    Quoting: "What did the President know and when did he know it?"
Like many persons in power, Trickie Dickie knew how to play games,
    His power scheme caught him in violations of the laws for campaigns!

There was also the scheming of Colonel North and G. Gordon Liddy,
    With sleazes like these, they were sucked up with old Trickie Dickie.
His family held their dignity that provided anchors for the President,
    But his resignation vacated the White House with them as resident.

Becoming a national leader comes with temptations to control power,
    This insidious addiction can be both conscious but also unconscious,
Leaders may assume they not only makes laws but are above them,
    A human obsession with power to control tempts to make laws bend.

Bush had trouble to stay within the laws, regulations and Constitution,
    His legal acumen was readily swayed by tricky lawyers for a solution.
His approval of torture of prisoners went overboard rationalizing,
    Both American citizens and global critics found him unsatisfying.

Bush also was lax about corporate practices and legal improprieties,
Big corporate power players dominated him to avoid key regulations.
With "w," corporations were not hurting, but they were hoarding,
Charles Blow surmised this gap for their common good was lacking.

"w" with Cheney and Rumsfeld invaded Iraq, Afghanistan weakened,
They did not even comply with their own label for fighting the Taliban.
Their code for the Afghan war was "Operation Enduring Freedom,"
By diverting to Iraq and Sadaam, they were not themselves "enduring."

Their misinterpretation of limited military intelligence was revealing,
They did not endure in Afghanistan, but they weakened Army fighting.
They did not comprehend that some peoples cannot endure freedom,
Without experience and behavioral control, persons are at loose ends.

"w" himself was enamored with being considered a war President,
His own insecure vanity became apparent when on an Aircraft Carrier.
"OPERATION COMPLETED" was flagrant evidence of misjudging,
"w" also showed up in an aircraft jumpsuit with also face grinning.

Pre-maturity can be characteristic of persons who are compensating,
"w's" display of being adulated, his vulnerability was not convincing.
The Taliban were not conceding but reassembled to become stronger,
Diverting military strength to Iraq lost our credibility with Allies again.

While "w" informed citizens that he possessed Christian commitment,
His lack of comprehending the nature of "freedom" was very evident.
Luther paradoxically balanced the two sides that "w" misunderstood,
"Freedom to serve" is the balance to "freedom from regulating rules."

Is there evidence that "w" or "Cheney" grasped the nature of paradox?
Their public comments were very superficial but by media sought out.
Can anyone find if they comprehended complex issues as paradoxical?
Nor penetrating grasp of conflict polarities for understanding issues?

Not only did the "w" team lack analytical skills for decision-making,
They made the plan to invade Iraq before intelligence was reporting.

So this "Team?" had made up their minds and looked for justification,
   Then they did not find any actual Iraq Weapons of Mass Destruction!

When the economic recession hit during his Presidential term,
   "w" deferred to cronies who protected their own financial concerns.
Naturally Big Boys in greedy financials make big profits their fete,
   "w" left the nation in a shambles of two wars with economic defeat.

He lost influence when he turned his decision to bankers and brokers,
   Back to Texas but not to his Crawford ranch but to Dallas comforters.
His Presidential Library is another campus "show piece" at S.M.U.,
   It was designed to protect his flawed heritage for "vulnerables" to view.

His appearances are limited to those with sympathy for his legacy,
   Historians are already assessing the values of his eight-year Presidency.
His experience and his perspectives had little value and currency,
   His two unfinished wars stand out as his impact on modern history.

CHAPTER 4: OBAMA<>BIDEN ADMINISTRATION

When Barack Obama became 44th President, a new era was launched,

His "Big Picture Perspectives" with not hastily decisions to be made.

This giant economy faced disaster that was already a Great Recession,

He was not a fast decision-maker but rather sought broad consensus.

His years of 2009 to mid-2011 are marked with multiple developments,

His persona is more mysterious as he is not transparently extroverted.

What is his Shadow is like is not clearly estimated at this early stage,

He is too complicated to readily profile that has not shown with age.

Yes, Obama is concerned with education as a highly achieving student,

He excelled at Harvard Law School to be the "Editor of Law Review!"

He is burdened with bad economic and educational decisions of Bush,

Recovering from ten years of regression, even now we have to rush.

It was clear that Obama had a wife who was an anchor for a leader!

Michelle is now highly educated and experienced as a front-runner!

Raising two daughters was a responsibility to take very seriously

She was obviously the anchor in Washington for their family.

The deep problems with horrendous symptoms are very deep-seated,

Wars and economic recession have had three decades with being fed.

The public was lacking perspectives with understandable limited views,

Confusing historical symptoms of problems without sensing causes.

The stark polarizations in Congress and the county made it impossible,

Learning compromise of differences so "Getting to Yes" was plausible.

The Tea Party's simple agenda was not a positive goals but negativity,

The grossly inexperienced new Congressmen already showed rigidity.

Four-year terms as elected officials presented a problem in democracy,

Office holders were so conscious of being re-elected there was hypocrisy.

They could not readily identify problems without already having positions,

So "short-term fixes" happened plus inability to do long-term solutions.

Obama was a young black law professor;

He showed us that he was also wiser.

He chose Biden as Vice-President;

He contributed to Obama's experience!

Obama knew when he did not know!

As he sought advice then to show.

He appointed to his own cabinet

For advice drawn from the internet.

Obama faced an economic crisis;

Financial banks over-extended.

This was a major accomplishment;

That also stabilized the government!

Obama also consulted with global leaders;

Many were impressed by his insights.

International issues needed attention;

This added to his comprehension.

Then he addressed a major challenge:

U.S. Health Care needed attention!

Yes, he knew how to make compromises;

This approach helped him in these crises.

Obama was faced with a Great Recession;

This one arose since the Great Depression!

America dealt with this as a major setback;

Citizens were in very bad markets!

Obama and Vice-President Biden

Had to learn new economic lessons.

Business people were not optimistic;

This became a challenge to politics.

The recovery was seen as amazing;

Indicated our nation as toughening.

Market resilience was also encouraging;

Helping citizens to engage in investing.

Obama-Biden showed leadership;

Americans inspired in citizenship!

Globally this was very essential

Humanity yearns for our potential!

"OBAMACARE" was then introduced;

Efforts made that poor were addressed.

This became a note able accomplishment

Tested by the opposition in the government!

Health care is a major issue in the United States;

Health Insurance tries to seek private big profits!

The health system had been very profitable

Much more than in the European cultures.

The Republican Party did challenges;

The Health Care Industry wanted edges.

For-profit corporations made election pledges.

Obamacare helped poor and those with illnesses.

There are three major issues in Health Policies;

These are best held in balance that is not easy.

One is "Access" to health care for citizens;

So that health care is available for persons.

A second issues deals with costs of care;

High costs go beyond what people can bare.

America's system has been very expensive;

But Government funding helps as a preventive.

A third is key for good care known as quality;

Patients deserve care to remain healthy!

America's health system does vary;

Obamacare did this carefully!

These policies are so very badly needed;

Obama did these wisely so it was handled.

Efforts to end it had been tried several times;

Americans benefited from these policies.

Obama also faced problems in the Middle East;

The tensions were high with these countries!

Vice-President Biden handled these issues;

These were brewing from the past crises.

PRESIDENTIAL TIMBER

Now to contrast what are improved expectations dealing with disparities,

The current stable of the out-of-power party is noticeably frustrating
.
"Where are the grown-ups?" who are both competent and also credible,

Tea Party Rightists seek press, money and attention almost unbearable.

Yes, we have Governors whose have records are less than enthralling,

Seeking visible popularity by attaching Washington while glamorizing.

When surface appearances get these lightweights surface appearances,

Is 2012 a beauty contest or a contest for those with top competencies?

Each rising announcement touts piety and then also what they oppose,

What they advocate is narrower domestic "flim-flam" without purpose.

The depth of analyzing causes of problems is readily assessed as shallow,

Soon they will attack each other when they are all in the rink together.

During eight years as incumbent, Obama faced many difficulties,

He was cool in demeanor as a statesman makes uncertain probabilities.

Some interpret his coolness as an "ivy league disdain" for commoners,

His articulations are measured making him opaque to the listeners.

He understandably "irritated the ire" of states' rights Southern advocates,

Distractions by deceivers planted seeds about his true citizenship as "birthers!"

Tea Party rebels tried to combine revolutionary war slogans and slaveholders,

Right extremists were imbalanced as unexamined economic supply-siders!

The Supreme Court's 2010 ruling of "freedom of money as speech was dubious,"

Unfortunately, "big-money" speakers dominated out of proportion as voters.

Not only have financial, insurance and pharmaceuticals given additives,

But defense contractors, farmers, labor and bankers have become addictive.

Candidates without backing from big money are easy to simply ignore,

Obama is supported by little people and big rollers competing for an encore.

Could he maintain balanced support from the broader center not extremists?

His poise in communications and sharp mind did continue his dreams!

Yes, Obama had noticeable vulnerabilities including his cool demeanor,

His stalling appears disengaged as people are not reflectively patient.

His middle ground negotiations were not seen as flashy on media,

Quick-fix movie clips on TV conditions voters for quick decisions.

Bush considered himself as a "Decider" but consequences are elusive,

Historical analysis is quickly discovering how many see Bush as abusive,

His smiles lubricated the limited insights that are now being revealed,

His VP was powerful as loose-gun whose influence is no longer concealed.

Americans are easily deceived by leaders whose piety is worn on their sleeve,

Religious values are essential with even deeper ethics and justice to conceive.

Watch out for dripping-juicy religious innuendo that is very calculated,

While many think our Founding Fathers were "disciples," such are deceived.

True and false prophets are difficult to distinguish right at the same time,

Eventual assessments reveal how often in slick media we are deceived.

Campaign managers contaminate our democracies with floods of trivia,

Election campaign managers of candidates can also set up straw persons.

What may be essential for Presidents now and into the foreseeable future?

Without attempting to prioritize, here are criteria for you to consider:

Capacities to intuitively and empirically seek the will of informed voters,

Balanced by skills to channel uninformed preferences into a better future!

A President and V-P benefit from engaging a range of global perspective,

This broad awareness based upon as many disciplines as could be feasible.

Diplomatic leadership to address unknown issues internationally is critical,

Creativity in both relationships and international policy issues are viable.

Capacities to listen patiently to diverse viewpoints of even narrow-minded,

Plus persuasive communication on complex problems while open-ended.

A wide range of abilities to address and convince many varied audiences,

With capacity to establish trustful relationships even at global distances.

The Presidential Office is extremely demanding seeking to find consensus,

Uncompromising Congressional Leaders can paralyze this fragile system.

Instant broadcasts to uninformed publics is obviously a major vulnerability,

Few leaders possess the stamina or ability to exude the demanding vitality.

ECONOMIC DISCREPANCIES AND DISPARITIES

Americans are viewed by others as both arrogant and exploitative;

How could foreigners even begin to questions our pure motives?

Are we not justified to protect our Allies so "What's the trouble?"

Quickly we learn that the world perceives us in our own bubble!

We are boisterous when displayed in the global public image;

As "Know-it-all" bragging, but we also have our baggage.

Whether it is true or not, is less than a productive question,

Psychologically human beings believe their own perception.

Americans display "Airs of Superiority" with our presence;

Others have feelings of inferiority compounded by accents.

Now if we are inconsiderate, exploitative and also audacious

We may be in our own small shell, thinking we are gracious.

Who imagines that Americans may also be greedy and loud?

In multi-fellowship of cultures, we often stand out in a crowd.

Americans are very honored but we are also disrespectful;

We would rather be perceived as wealthy and beautiful!

Disparities between the wealthy and extremely poor are known,

Most cultures have similar discrepancies so we are not alone.

The enormous inequities of riches and poverty are very obvious;

Americans and others have failed to correct this as audacious!

Who would care to consider Americans as boldly controlling?

Other people see that we are actually engaged in patrolling.

We justify that we appear strong rather than to look weak;

Such displays of power are different from another's peak.

Why does the Egyptians revolution prompt these reflections?

Are we on a corrupt path rather than the founder's directions?

Democracy is not perfect, so why must we look at ourselves?

New fledgling democracies need other models for themselves.

Has America a perfect vision of the writers of the Constitution?

Perhaps that is need for reassessments for further evolution?

Will other people want to be free to handle these incongruities?

Do democracies have ready corrections to aid our continuities?

Self-examination is a challenge when we think we are right;

While external perceivers could also see we are not so bright.

The rebellions in the Middle East do raise many questions;

If American a model for change in our own exceptionalism?

When Americans try to comprehend "how we see as we are seen,"

Is a mirror or is a rebellion necessary to see what we have been?

What feedback channels designed for gaining more insight?

To get attention to reflect may require motivation of fright!

The United Nations is a forum where diplomatic exchanges occur,

Interactions function effectively when all parties will observe.

When Americans encounter the coalitions that are protective,

Do we listen carefully with respect to gain other perspective?

American power includes its own military, economic and political;

Provide unequalled leverage on vulnerable populations unequally.

Transnational corporations are more influential than nations,

Restraints for markets can be exploited without regulations.

Controls are more effective if wealthy collective are responsible,

These obligations are interpreted whether moral or ethical.

Unbridled firms have impressions either positive or negative,

Interpreting cultural standards can also be very subjective.

Effective global courts enforce provisions of contracts are limited,

Exploiting weak contractors is consequential by being subjugated.

Perspective for fairness is varied and also culturally conditioned,

Outcomes are uncertain for negotiations that may not be sound.

But national images are highly influenced by very fluid factors,

Impressions are lasting though subjective and elusive reflectors.

As negative impressions are provoked these are difficult to correct.

Consequently, cultural reputations may result in lack of respect.

Will Americans be aware that we are seen by others differently?

Will we continue to use our power imposing it indiscriminately?

Current generations have disparities between powerful and weak,

Will we see the world differs from what we say or how we speak.

Other global citizens perceive varieties of images on television,

They may see the rich and glamorous without discrimination.

Media engages viewers with impressions that both can make,

Viewers may misperceive us until traveling where they awake.

Our retreating unforgivably lacks concern for the unemployed,

Ideals of equality are suffering from disparities in fair wealth.

Immigrants are marginalized when they are treated as scapegoats,

Our hospitality as neighbors I diminished keeping them afloat.

Inside American there are tensions approaching that are angry,

If leaders do not respond constructively, rebellion is a possibility.

When our own government is controlled by the very wealthy,

Are we a plutocracy or do we have the ideals of a democracy?

Power will corrupt people at any level of social structure,

Insensitivity is compounded to be possibly destructive.

Will American citizens regain a sense of healthy culture?

Rebellion seen in Egypt and Tunisia are clues of rupture.

Powerful leaders are impervious to cries for more sensitivity.

Oppressed see causes controlled by powers without elasticity.

Rebellions stir up voices through anger, violence and vices,

Unaware controllers of politically powerful make choices.

Do citizens realize government is "OF-BY and FOR the PEOPLE?"

Rather than "FOR the RICH," "BY CRONIES" or for the feeble.

The lessons from the revolutions in the Middle East are ominous,

Reflective Americans may have opportunity to be magnanimous!

CHAPTER 5: TRUMP'S BUMPS

As complex developments do emerge;

Trump's symptoms mentally did occur!

His declarations claimed wire-tapping!

Accusing Obama of serious medaling!

Evidence to support this was not found!

But Trump's suspicions have continued!

His own party has found no evidence!

But the public was being held in suspense!

These developments prompted investigation!

Raising hypotheses that needed explanation!

His own symptoms had patterns of paranoia

"Alternative facts" could not be deployed!

Further diagnostic procedures were needed

Trump's accusations of Obama were weird!

Symptoms of paranoia by a global leader,

Could prompt crises across the whole world!

America during Trump's leadership became:

Less free! Less equal! And deeper in debt!

Much more divided into bad factions!

Swampier and dirtier and deader![6]

Trump appointed many Judges rated as

"Not qualified" by American Bar Association.

25,000 false or misleading statements.

National Debt increased by seven trillion $!

He had affection of N. Korea's Kim!

He also admired Russia's Putin;

He was hostile to minorities;

Racial groups and women.

---

6   Packer, G., January-February, 2021,"The Legacy of Donald Trump," <u>The Atlantic."</u>

Truth to him did not matter;

Trust in him was degraded!

His reputation did decline;

So he served just one term!

TRUMP'S MIND!

Mental developments compound under stress!

Trump's staff were also placed in a quandary!

Who could check the President's accusations?

His cabinet and staff faced tough situations!

Who might a President talk with confidentially?

Some other leaders have messed up historically!

Hitler, Stalin, Wilson and Mao had personalities

Precluding them from handling crises personally!

Were there clues about Trump's mental processes?

Both Trump and citizens were under stresses!

Unpredictable outcomes could be expected

But citizens chose a President they elected!

These recent developments need attention!

By both American and also global citizens!

Perceptive professionals could be helpful

To preclude outcomes that were unexpected!

THE ART OF THE DEAL!

In this book, Trump advocated wheeling and dealing!

He claimed to sell like his property empire wielding!

"TRUTHFUL HYPERBOLE" called for understanding!

He had his own strategy to get the public believing.

"THE BIGGEST! plus THE GREATEST! SPECTACULAR!"

Trump promoted his sales to be very outstanding by far!

His success rested on a talent: "BAMBOOZLING RUBES!"

Persuading people that he was playing by the rules!

He found the gambit or how to convince people!

This did then become the deals in real estate!

As a salesman who greatest product was himself!

Leading customers to be the envy of every else!

Trump slapped his name on things like skyscrapers!

Plus his casinos, golf courses and Trump University!

What looked attractive made it very convincing!

Except he had come short at eventually delivering!

Then as President wanting to repeal "Obama Care!"

This challenge raised issues he was not aware!

He wanted people on "government" aid to work;

He promoted this goal so no one would shirk!

Health Care financing is very complicated!

The patient, health insurance and government!

His parties' 1st plan would leave millions uninsured!

"Worst-off-Citizens" then before Trump started!

MORE PENDING QUESTIONS!

Was Trump influenced by obsessions?

His comments became revelations!

It was apparent that he was a controller!

Pronouncements made him sound bolder!

Trump just loved to say: "You're Fired!"

On his own TV show, it was also required!

His "thrust-out jaw" accented statements!

In power, he loved to make pronouncements!

Trump acted like a "King," not President!

What about Congress and Supreme Court?

Did he withstand this balance of powers?

This democracy was not made for a dictator!

He then also had some "Come-Uppance!"

He could not govern from some distance!

Sharing power was his own difficulty!

As he learned his role in a democracy!

Trump was soon to be "Over-Exposed!"

More citizens saw what he did not know!

Skeptics and supporters did have opposition!

His promises did not to do, came into fruition!

Poor and vulnerable did became victims!

When Trump did not fulfill predictions!

As the wealthy benefited in resources

Polarization he expressed in discourses!

Trump's proposed 2018 budget was disturbing!

Programs he cut and those also supporting.

Military benefits and social programs suffered!

Wealthy got tax breaks; the poor were losers!

Healthy benefits were also being reduced!

And public education without any boost!

The State Department also had to struggle

To represent the United States in trouble!

Trump's own statement were puzzles!

Without evidence for confirmations!

His staff did struggle for evidence

Particularly global warming science!

Some substantive proofs were to be expected;

Unsupported comments were challenged!

Conflict management was also necessary!

To discover direction while in quandaries!

TRUMP'S SNAGS

Trump typically claimed to be very smart!

Overshadowing others from the start!

He was caught in "nettles of obsession!"

In his own personal pre-occupations!

He was insecure about his competencies!

Including his mentalities and fantasies!

He claimed himself to be very smart!

Protecting himself had become an art!

His models while growing up had influence;

Who had an impact by providing guidance?

These did include his Father, Fred T. Trump,

Plus Roy Cohn, Senator McCarthy's chump!

Some authors saw Trump as very insecure!

Suggesting that he wanted validation love!

Did people notice-that-he never stayed quiet!

Pre-occupied by making his own comments!

Trump was diverted by attacking President Obama!

Claiming that he invaded Trump's own electronics!

Even when no evidence had even been produced

Trump persisted in whatever he had claimed!

Trump avoided ever becoming a victim!

He attacked others in order to lick them!

He liked to imitate Churchill's sternness

He was obsessed by showing he was earnest!

Trump readily used lies to defend himself!

He claimed not to be influenced by Putin!

Trump played on the fantasies of people!

But did not want others to be his equal!

Leonhardt[7] saw Trump as a Pavlovian!

Observing that Trump used challenges;

Responded to stimuli with quick reactions!

As President, he did disturb other nations!

---

[7]   Leonhardt, D., (March 20, 2017) The New York Times.

GUESS WHO?

Who provided us with his self-images?

Obviously, his own ego was self-inflated!

His personal pride was similarly excessive!

America was worried about his damages!

As he encountered the global dangers,

His own over-confidence was unrealistic!

His business experience was not in politics!

He could not control major global affairs!

"HUBRIS" described his own arrogance!

His frequent displayed over-confidence!

Every day he revealed his own self-pride!

Attacking those on the opposite side!

GLOBAL AFFAIRS

Global leaders did encounter him!

He had limits in being diplomatic!

Likely they did see him as egocentric!

There were differences in politics!

Did he challenge their interests?

He had limited skills in viewpoints,

This probably impeded his offenses;

As he did also become defensive!

Did he not try dealing with Middle East?

Many complex religions there do exist!

These issues for millennia are complex

Many have hostility toward the West!

How did he address global warming?

Pressure did influence his decisions!

Did he see scientific recommendations?

Or draw upon his own intuitions?

DOMESTIC ISSUES

America's internal problems are complex!

It is difficult to predict what to expect!

A wide range of problems do now exist!

And more crises are very likely to persist!

He promised to increase employment!

He leaned on businesses to raise jobs!

But technology replaces many roles!

Obviously manufacturing also decreases!

Health care is also very expensive!

Culling "Obama Care" was ridiculous!

"Fee-for-Service" is a major problem!

Making difficulties to find solutions!

It was doubtful he comprehended this!

He shunned the European models!

His had limits in health affairs!

This was revealed in proposals!

POLITICAL COMPLEXITIES

America's democracy is admirable!

Political compromises are essential!

The Supreme Court and also Congress

Balance proposals of the President!

Trump was very unaccustomed to Boards!

Government has needs for approvals!

Negotiations represent many interests

These complex processes take patience!

Elections complicate decision-making!

Gender issues now are awakening!

His masculinity was challenged!

What did the public then discover?

TRUMP DENIED DEFEAT

Trump denied defeat in the 2020 Election;

He did persist to the point of dejection.

He insisted that votes be recounted.

In five states, results were doubted.

In Michigan, votes he could not accept;

Trump assumed that he won the bets.

In Pennsylvania he questioned results;

He insisted the outcomes with doubts.

In Arizona and Nevada, he did not win;

Voters wondered if he would give in!

In Georgia, he hoped 11,000 votes change;

To the public, he seemed very strange.

Trump had real difficulty facing facts!

This showed his own bizarre acts.

The solid evidence was unaccepted;

Trump presumed Biden was defeated.

He also doubted temperature increases;

This showed lack of climate sciences.

Evidence was denied in Trump's mind;

He acceptance of facts was way behind.

MANY UNKNOWNS

Curious persons notice unknowns!

Hoping that evidence will be shown!

What was his own learning curve?

Could he zig-zag or even swerve?

Did Trump seek more advice?

Rather than throwing the dice!

Global decisions can be irreversible!

His mysteriousness was undesirable!

Did he become a fox or a wolf?

Or did he then remain very aloof?

He remained very unpredictable!

Nuclear issues are so controversial!

Mysteriousness could be unwise!

Global issues do not like surprises!

Humans hope life will be predictable!

Unknowns are not likely to be reliable!

WHO KNOWS?

Humans prefer what is predictable!

Hoping political leaders are capable!

Unpredictable leaders can make risks

About who should continue to persist!

Unfolding decisions will be revealed!

Eventually these cannot be concealed!

Research can be helpful to a degree,

In time, we will then also get to see!

Mr. Mysterious revealed his leadership!

Did he become a person to worship?

The future years will be a revelation!

Of how he led America as a nation!

TRUMP'S GRADED FOR HIS TERM

This was my report for Trump's 1ˢᵗ School Year:

His own grades emerged just as you fear!

As U.S. citizens accountable to you!

We can see his grades for review!

His quality of work had been "Devolving!"

In many classes, he was very Diverting!

In fact, we see that his was Degrading!

His public comments were Disgusting!

More of his "D's" were for his Deceiving!

He also tried to master his Deflecting!

But these attempts were Denouncing!

His terminology was also Distracting!

He likewise did some Diversion!

At times, words showed Decimation!

People wondered about his Delusions!

Plus put downs were Dehumanization!

Trump's reactions also revealed Denial!

In fact, his comments were Dreadful!

Often, he praised himself as a Dealer!

While others see him as a Dreamer!

Occasionally he could be Devilish!

But listeners saw him as Derelict!

A few noticed his Debauchery!

Others noticed his Depravity!

He fired people he Dismisses!

Others turned out Depressed!

Did he himself have Delusions?

Or was this his skill in Deflation?

This may relate to his Defaming!

In order to make others Disturbing?

Opponents also saw him Disagreeing

And his crude words were Debasing!

We did not want Trump to be Desperate!

So how could we close his grade report?

Would we provide an encouraging word?

Would a "D+" even help him go onward?

CHAPTER 6: TRUMP'S: EMERGENCE OR EMERGENCY?

In 2007-08, there were incited reactions!

The T-Party ten gained its own traction!

Suppressed antagonism also emerged!

Prejudicial reason, indirectly expressed!

While enthusiasm arose for Obama,

Racial hostility became a socio-drama!

Many voters displayed prejudice indirectly

Expressing their own objections fervently!

Yes, Barack had real Republican resistance;

He pursued responsibilities with persistence!

His supporters were often openly criticized!

A large number of voters were disguised.

This was not publicly acknowledged clearly.

As citizens vote their preferences privately!

Perceptive persons could penetrate facades!

Even though they might openly show applause!

TRUMP'S BLESSINGS!

Discontent undergirded Trump's victory!

His own negatives were overlooked hardly!

Reacting to the lethargic long experience

Overlooking Trump's lack of conscience!

Was his 2016 victory prompted by change?

While tolerated, he was also strange!

His obvious narcissism was a challenge

Was his own win downloading revenge?

His staff was trying to use alternate facts!

Were these not unusual inaccurate acts?

When facts have different accuracies

Was this country due for catastrophes?

How can the public here and worldwide?

Determine what are facts or inaccuracies?

Manufactured data were very dubious!

Could the public have been oblivious!

Would Trump recognize racial conflicts?

As white who refused to rent to blacks?

Had he ever visited anyone in prison?

Did he know about racial discrimination?

What did he know about public education?

He went to private schools plus his children.

His Education Secretary who privatized!

Did Trump know schools in real crises?

A critical item was vast military expenditures!

Political economies and human relations!

Protection of America is very important

Did Trump know what was significant?

Allies needed to know Trump's commitments

What did "America First" take to implement?

Global crises are typically very unpredictable

But this world wanted America to be reliable!

Trump himself had never been in the military!

How aware was he of serving on active duty?

Service personnel naturally have uncertainty

As Commander-in-Chief, did he serve reliably?

GLOBAL HUMANITY

Was Trump versed about Asia and Africa?

What did he know about South America?

Just how would he address crises globally?

Was his ego challenged psychologically?

Could Trump have suffered from denial?

Global warming was for him a trial!

Facts to him apparently were relative,

Reality may have been to him subjective!

For the Middle East, Trump needed more education!

He wanted American Embassy moved to Jerusalem!

To the Palestinians, this would become a crisis!

For the Israelis, this move did have prices!

The whole Middle East is a tinder box!

Explosive conflicts were easily erupted!

This illustrated Trump's lack of perception,

About global issues that resulted in eruption!

Trump denied any higher temperatures!

He supported coal industry's carbon ventures!

He also disputed scientific research evidence!

Regressing into his own defensive trenches!

Trump had slim awareness of research!

Ready to leave life in compromising lurch!

Other nations recognized these crises

While he neglected the costly prices!

People are the most important resource!

Many do rely on earth sciences research!

Evidence is crucial for making decisions!

Humanity cannot rely on just his opinions!

PARTICIPATION OR ISOLATION?

Trump's apprehensions came out as fear!

He did express disagreement with sneers!

He did not affirm scientific global warming

Instead, he relied on simplistic bullying.

He also displayed critical Xenophobia

Particularly aimed at Islamophobia!

Immediately crowds started objections;

Rallies occurred in the world and this nation!

When Donald Trump dealt with criticism;

He often responded with corny witticisms!

Attacking persons without understanding

Key issues that needed comprehending!

His style or exchange was not polished!

International contacts may be abused!

Making personal attacks had resistance

Particularly when he expressed insistence!

HOW ABOUT RESTRAINTS?

Restraint is a concept to learn about

Would Trump ever learn not to shout?

His boisterous comments were boastful

Highlighting his own need to be awful!

Had he ever been modest with restraint?

Or was he noted for making complaints?

His styles of conversation were puzzling

Making difficulties for those wondering!

His tone was like that of a Commander

As it was not his very own banner!

Observers noticed this very quickly,

Noticing his stanches were prickly!

How was his style received globally?

Would his-come-uppance occur?

Hopefully this was not a disaster!

Was his need to try to act superior?

TRUMP'S TAX RETURNS

For financial confidence to be gained

His own tax returns were not provided!

His reluctance did raise more suspicion

Because many people knew this tradition!

However, Trump used his choice to resist

Suggesting he did not have to account!

While government taxes needed attention;

His own finances also needed comprehension!

He did not have awareness of USA budgets!

He was not aware of revenues and also debts!

Full accountability to citizens can be imposed

His management of finances was exposed!

Running his real estate was very different

Although he did know about bankruptcy!

Public finances involve 330+ million citizens

Who did tire of their President's witticisms?

DEPTH?

Trump's depth of comprehension was pitiful!

His surface assessments were deplorable!

Many Americans failed to understand

Obvious shallowness shown by this man!

Examples included his estimates of crowds!

His inauguration witnesses were small

But he raised questions of their estimates

His hoped that there were big mistakes!

Did Trump have depth into introspection?

His popular votes he called into question!

Then his staff raised doubts of registration!

Because he did not accept tallies in election!

Initial assessments saw his superficiality

He also questioned research scientifically!

Citizens quickly noticed lack of depth!

Dependability was in the state of bereft!

BREADTH?

What could global humanity have expected?

So were foreigners treated with respect?

Suspicions of Trump were very apparent

By large numbers of Muslims and Mexicans!

His own cabinet had narrow perspectives!

From Attorney General to Sec. of Education!

His advisory staff was also very limited

To assess global issues and domestic!

So what was our future to become?

Developments were very hard to sum!

So much of the world was in turmoil!

But the future may have quagmire!

"MAKE AMERICA GREAT AGAIN!"

Trump's campaign's own slogan!

His posturing became a problem

His bargaining expected concessions!

PRONOUNCEMENTS OF DIPLOMACY?

Trump's personal language was crude!

With women, he was especially crude!

Did Donald Trump have no decency?

Where was he trained in diplomacy?

One-way statements are not conversation!

Could he learn to use more persuasion?

His own remarks were an embarrassment,

Thinking he could make pronouncements!

His selection of cabinet lent to problems!

Did he listen to their sincere comments?

Or was "Group-Think" then practiced?

Seeking affirmation rather than insights?

Without contrary feedback being provided

Many of his views were not evaluated!

How long before he discovered critiques?

Rather than often discrediting the source!

CHAPTER 7: TRUMP'S NEW QUAGMIRE

Trump's style was to be on trial?

He relished giving orders and signing!

Were Presidential Orders appropriate?

These regal acts appeared on television!

Repeatedly Trump displayed narcissism!

Dramatically signing a big document!

Again this portrayed his egocentrism

As if everybody watches and listens!

He loved the role of an executive!

The "Decision-Maker" giving orders!

He wore blue suits to be positive,

Full attire in the role of "Manager!"

One order of his did meet resistance!

Citizens expected to receive immigrants!

However, Trump identified seven nations;

Did he not want to admit these citizens?

FURTHER CONCERNS

Trump's demands were to be tested!

"Take out Terrorists!" "Outmatch them!"

Expanded our nuclear forces as a threat!

Heightened tensions in order to outlast!

Did he appreciate China's positions?

Or Russia's historically great traditions?

Trump's posturing did result in problems!

He did not have abilities to solve them.

His four years had numerous unknowns!

Did Trump recognize what he would be shown?

His own capacity for denial was very fragile!

He presented the world with his own style!

As more persons go to Washington

Marching with Trump as Republicans.

Then new pending questions arise!

Why did he lead us into crises?

Did he know that he was in danger?

Could he also swim as a beginner?

Messy swamps are houses of snakes;

Did he try also to make earthquakes?

Trump was accustomed to hotels

Ordering the help with his yells!

Then he lived in "The White House!"

But it did not have an outhouse!

His quagmire has grown even higher

As deep as the Washington spire!

His cruiser did not have a dock!

Second impeachment so he walked!

GETTING IN DEEPER

America speculated if he lasted!

Trump soon did have to gasp!

He thought of handling bankruptcies;

We saw how he handled the economy!

Wars erupt quickly in remote places!

Sometimes are old antagonistic cases!

If he ever should decide to go nuclear,

Big tragedies damage all hemispheres!

Nuclear War results in huge atrocities!

It would heighten some old polarities!

Did Trump already have awareness?

About how to initiate peace processes?

How could he bring enemies together?

To reduce old hostilities as negotiators?

He did know how to fire up tensions;

How might he manage new dissensions?

Trump did not affirm global warming!

His grasp of the sciences was not assuring!

With global power, our future was troubling

!

How huge was his deficit in new learning?

His propensities to fire opponents

Heightened risks for tragic moments!

He could be a "high risk" global leader,

Antagonizing animosities into disaster!

TRUST

How could Trump generate trust?

Beyond people beholden to persist?

His marriages indicated more trouble

As he arranged to live in a bubble!

He tried to retain economic controls,

Intimidating their bodies and souls!

He's confronted with global powers

Who were different than hotel towers!

Power tempted leaders to extend control

Unconscious factors erupted to be bold!

Trump did not handle needs of his ego

Ignoring limits of what could be legal!

His familiarity with the constitution,

Had severe gaps for comprehension!

Did he accept advice for decisions?

Honoring what had preceded him?

Additional campaigning was bewildering;

Candidates declared by self-nominating!

They were not endorsed by their party;

Thrusted themselves so irregularly!

Initially candidates addressed key issues;

Proposing solutions without the funds.

Quickly they made personal attacks;

Degrading opponents without facts!

Aggressiveness diverted from issues;

Belittling soon became degrading!

Debate levels needed to be elevated;

Strengths and weaknesses respected!

Bullying behind opponents backs;

Official rules violated without facts!

Humiliating candidates for fighting;

Showmanship was not enlightening!

Fear initiated his tactics of bullying;

Bullies think they are competing.

The attacks often were weaknesses

Disclosing limits of appearances!

Bluffing was a type of showmanship;

Covering actions that lack depths!

Bluffers are full of wind that blows

Watch what direction hot air flows!

Disrespect soon showed up bullying;

Tearing down was easier than building.

Shallowness was so quickly disclosed;

And loud attacks become so crude!

TV appearances were for "surface;"

Not revealing under these facades!

These hid bullies own vicious cores;

Not solutions but resorting to wars!

Insults do not gain positive results;

Instead, they revealed personal faults!

Rising above negativity was really vital;

Providing public more positive signals!

Belittling opponents had opposite effects;

Within time, they began to fight back!

This hostility consequently did backfire;

Users might be labelled as big liars!

The more foreign things you forbid;

The less safe your world becomes!

This Xenophobic paradox was not insight

Rather it came from being afraid of fright!

Bluffing can be another strategy;

Misleading opponents with mystery!

As a tactic in negotiations and cards;

It can turn into lessening of regards!

Bluffers become known as puffers;

In time this is uncovered to voters.

A wolf trying to blow the house down;

Residents found him bluffing around!

Hot winds can make windmills turn;

And cause water waves to churn!

But bluffers make citizens quake;

So that nations are less than a state!

Crude candidates could also disrupt;

They launch campaigns to upset!

With limited ideas what was involved?

Resulted in confusion but not solved!

Some candidate can also disrupt;

They get in campaigns just to upset!

With limited ideas what is involved;

Results in confusion that is not solved!

Democracies are vulnerable to disruptions;

They are cousins of what is called bluffers!

But neither of them will last very long;

Seeking attention for their own song!

Why do we tolerate these people?

Is freedom exploited just for turmoil?

Democracy is vulnerable to exploitation

What system is better for our nation?

DDD: Displacement, Denial and Distortion;

By resorting to tactics out of proportion!

Voters can only be fooled part of the time;

Soon critics will see through their slime!

America faces key issues currently!

Many are domestic; others globally!

Serving for connection as a bridge,

Sometimes America is upon a ridge!

Bridging Europe and Eastern Asia,

Also connecting with South America!

Concerned about China and Russia!

And the largest democracy, India!

America manages values and interests!

Pondering roles in the Middle East!

Challenges between Sunnis and Shiites.

How might we ever facilitate peace?

Israelis and Palestinians in tension!

Afghanistan and Iran apprehensions;

Pakistan battling neighbor, India;

All attention of Russia and China!

Concerns in Africa and South America!

Internal strife occurring in North Africa!

Likewise, Civil Wars and Old Autocracies

Trying to cultivate new Democracies!

Interests and values are in conflict!

Managing these is like a big trick!

Currently, we have United Nations

Global concerns and organized regions!

AMERICA IN THE 21ST CENTURY

How did Trump handle responsibilities?

How will freedom be managed effectively?

Governments differs from businesses,

Being faced with very different issues!

Trump was confronted with difficulties!

Can he evaluate alternatives effectively?

Both domestically and internationally!

Governments have problems officially!

Complex conflicts need reconciliation!

Beyond vast troubles between nations!

Political economies and human relations!

To arrive peaceful and fair among nations!

A President represents the United States!

Trump was engaged in talks and debates!

His learning curve needed to grow quickly!

Nations want justice internally-internally!

PLANETARY CHALLENGES

Very quickly there are civil wars!

But there are even more chores!

Some are now very complicated!

Requiring treaties to be negotiated

Global Temperature is an example!

Whether our human efforts are ample.

Immediate agreements are essential!

For human being to reach potentials

Trump denied the higher temperatures;

He supported the coal industry's carbon ventures.

He also disputed scientific research evidence;

Regressing into his own defensive trench.

Trump had slim awareness of research,

Ready to leave life in compromising lurch.

Other nations recognized pressing crises,

While he neglected to address costly prices!

People are the most important resource,

Many do rely on Earth Sciences research.

Evidence is crucial for making decisions;

Humanity cannot rely on just opinions!

Restraint is a concept to learn about,

Did Trump ever learn not to shout?

His boisterous comments were boastful;

Highlighting his own need to be dreadful.

Has he ever been modest without restraint?

Or was he noted for making complaints?

His style of conversation was puzzling

Making difficulties for those wondering!

His tone was like that of a Commander;

Highlighting his very own banner.

Observers noticed this very quickly;

Noticing his stanches were prickly.

How was his style received globally?

Did he try to relate as friendly?

Hoping this would not be a disaster;

Was this his need to try to act superior?

He readily criticized Obama's program;

He did so facing many new problems!

His Health Care plan was not tested;

Offered to the public without being tried.

Trump's own party tried to be supportive

His Health Care ideas seemed abortive.

This major issue illustrated his approach

His Administration needed a new coach!

Consensus was necessary to develop support;

His poll numbers were under 44% public reports.

Uncertainties indicated Americans were divided;

This is less than previous Presidents recorded!

Crowds may assemble to cheer temporarily;

Was Trump able to keep up his popularity?

American leadership was needed internationally;

Otherwise, a vacuum attracts others quickly!

Trump's party could not defeat "Obamacare!"

So they promised to try again, if they dare.

Low taxes are also another legislative item;

Hoping that a legislative majority was with them.

WHAT CRISES MIGHT OCCUR?

This open-ended question became speculative;

Interrogations can be negative or positive.

It is essential for foresee crises as serious;

Any anticipating issues is not mysterious.

Key political and economic problems occur;

Both social and international issues emerge.

Seasoned leaders anticipate what is ahead,

Therefore, tough issues must be studied!

Diplomatic negotiations and Russian connections;

Conflicts with ISIS, North Korea, Southwest Asians.

Congressional leaders, Democrats and Republicans;

Military and nuclear problems, ethical violations.

Nuclear weapons are naturally ominous!

Both for us in war plus their maintenance!

As they get older, they are more dangerous;

Careful precautions are needed to be prominent!

These weapons are wanted by global terrorists;

Therefore, even more dangers will then exist.

America's President has big responsibilities;

In learning how to make decisions carefully!

These types of wars can be sub-national;

Peace organizations are rarely global.

Established states are not their models;

Confined battles are more limited than wars!

Humanity needs to have more confidence,

In Leaders who govern with evidence!

Such power cannot be under-estimated;

For well-being of humanity world-wide!

Erratic global policies need attention;

So that there are well-considered options.

Erroneous decisions are also unforgiveable;

Nothing about nuclear warfare is trivial!

Another challenge is over-population!

Cooperation needed by people and nations!

Adequate food is now a major challenge!

Conflicts and wars motivate resolutions!

Over 200 million already in migrations!

No longer identified as citizens of nations!

Over 22 million are now seen as refugees!

Desperate adults and children among these!

Who will provide leadership for solutions?

Advanced nations are now in expectations!

Human Rights require good and protection!

These are challenges needing progression!

Humanitarian needs are in the forefront!

Privileged nations have these to confront!

May Americans address these promptly!

Requiring human services and empathy.

Americans are confronted with decisions;

Our nation is undergoing new revisions.

The Trump Administration was ominous;

Like an untamed animal is boisterous!

Yes, revelations of policies are showing;

Fears of polarizations are now growing.

Appointments by Trump were bewildering;

Extremists internally did begin serving!

Worldviews are now becoming narrower;

Trump was paying off his own supporters.

A number had very limited perspectives;

Indebted to special interest investments.

Fears prompt very powerful emotions;

Domestic fears do launch commotions!

Hatred of one's enemies and oppositions;

This can prompt international tensions!

The Middle East is a hotbed of trouble;

Trump's views of ISIS were disreputable!

He had limits in understanding cultures;

His development had narrow experiences!

His views of Muslims were very hostile!

Precluding views of respect as mutual.

His positions of permitting immigration

Festered negative international relations!

CHAPTER 8: DOCTOR OF THE SOUL

The term "SOUL" is very comprehensive

"The Whole Person!" designated inclusive.

Soul includes the tangible and intangible:

Mind-Body-Life-Spirit-Immortality-Integrity.

Greek "psyche" is translated as SOUL!

"Psyche Doctor" is a Doctor of SOULS!

Healer includes Ministry and Psychology.

Contrast Physician of the "physical body."

A Ph.D. requires an original dissertation,

Including scientific research and analysis!

Classical languages are also integrating,

Plus an oral defense of research findings.

"Doctor of the Soul" describes Psychology,

Integrating the relations of soul and body!

A body does not include a personal soul,

As an intangible dimension of the spiritual.

A Pastor engages in functions of ministry,

A Physician's focus is upon the visible body.

Physicians do not heal Soul and the Mind,

Ministers focus on spirituality and liturgy.

Healing "The Whole Person" is integrative,

Therapeutic approaches are more inclusive.

A Soul Doctor is comprehensively involving,

Including birth, living, nurturing and dying.

"Soul Sisters" describes very special women,

Thinking alike with similar feelings and emotions.

"Soul Brothers" connect in similar activities,

Comrades in teamwork and like-mindedness.

Spiritual experiences are felt deep in Souls,

    Words may not adequately describe these bonds.

Soul relations profoundly connect so uniquely,

    Special teamwork jointly is valued very highly.

"Saving Souls" is nurtured by Evangelism,

    This goal is commendable and misleading.

Salvation is God's Gift of Grace not earned,

    Human efforts are not efficacious for merit.

Gratitude is appropriate to being responsive,

    Prompting us to express being appreciative!

God gives to faithful recipients graciously,

    As we receive his Generous Love joyfully.

We are created as body, mind, spirit and Soul,

    Integrated in "personhood as unique beings!"

In social relationships expressing "I-Thou,"[8]

    So that personhood in society can blossom!

---

[8]   Buber., M., <u>I-THOU.</u>

CONSTRUCTIVE MANAGEMENT
OF SHADOWS

Human personality can be balanced;

Partly done by becoming explained;

Along with insights by supporters

Thereby shedding light on Shadows!

Without help, Shadows are devious

Because they are not obvious!

"Un-enlightenment" is dangerous;

Because Shadows are cantankerous.

Helpful persons are dear friends

Likewise, are one's teammates!

Of course, so are our spouses;

As well as close colleagues!

There are sources for explanations;

A reliable source is true religion!

A personal can raise real questions

Oneself may then do more reflections!

It is better to be enlightened;

Then to become very frightened.

This facilitates more contribution;

As the Ego-Shadow have reunion!

Personality traits reach to one's Shadow;

To be broadened and not remain narrow.

"Openness to enlarged new experiences"[9]

Reduces the "Ego-Shadow" distances!

Such personalities are integrated;

Instead of Ego-Shadow distanced.

They are agreeable to movement

Plus helping a person be resilient!

---

9   Goldberg, L., 1992, "The development of markers for Big-Five factor structures, Psychological Assessment 41.

A helpful quality is openness;

Opening a person to closeness!

Such personality is more holistic;

Facilitating one to be positivistic!

A Shadow often is negativistic

This reflects being a critic.

Some persons are neurotic

As well as being patriotic!

Integrative persons are conscientious

They avoid being too pretentious!

The Shadow can be malicious,

Hidden rather than obvious!

SHADOW'S EDUCATIONAL VALUE

A person's Shadow has an educational role;

We can learn from it when we are bold!

Our Shadow may expand our Persona![10]

---

[10]   Ford, D., 2010, <u>The Shadow Effect,</u> Harper and Row.

This confrontation requires definite bravery

We should not expect it to come out clearly.

Our Shadow helps us act compassionately!

As we mine into the deep parts of personality

Our darker side will benefit from honesty,

We should not expect it to be lovely!

Our Shadow is an important component;

This discovery becomes a key moment!

We may be tempted to try postponement.

On the other hand, we can embrace our Shadow

Because the Shadow helps us to be empowered!

By rounding us out rather than to be hidden.

This impacts our insights and our actions;

This may embolden one's future direction.

The Shadow can facilitate our imagination!

When a person does not recognize their Shadow;

As it continues to lurk; It does not stay fallow!

And one's personality remains somewhat narrow.

A Shadow that is hidden is unpredictable;

Undisclosed, it may even engage in ridicule!

This could be quite a saddening spectacle!

COLLECTIVE SHADOWS

Dark Shadows are not only personal

They are collective beyond individuals.

This is parallel to collective unconscious;

Often hidden from conscious awareness!

Societies have these as a challenge;

Particularly when tempted by revenge.

Now these collective Shadows are hidden;

Bursting forth into sudden eruptions.

Americans may hide a Shadow secretly;

Developed defensively and offensively!

This was the Atomic Bombs from WW II.

Nuclear weapons are more awesome.

Atomic Bombs brought WW II to an end!

After over 100,000 Japanese were killed!

These horrible losses were unfortunate;

The whole war was very inhumane!

Europeans and Pacific Theaters of wars!

As a pre-adolescent, I remember clearly;

My brother whom my family loved dearly

Flew missions over Japan patriotically!

Atomic bombs came out of research;

Scientists did these research projects.

Russia and USA have huge stockpiles!

Plus a few antagonists and allies!

Few citizens have much awareness;

All this is a very secret business!

Fortunately, there are nuclear controls;

Other nations may develop these goals.

Human beings have dangerous weapons!

Committed military personnel guard them!

My own awareness was an eye-opener

Now I will briefly describe this for readers.

An Air Force Officer with top security clearances;

An Assistant Base Adjutant with scientists.

I had responsibilities to secure documents;

Charged with Top Secret requirements.

Our Base tested weapons in the Pacific;

Colleagues followed the nuclear clouds

That drifted in the high atmosphere.

Fortunately, no accidents did appear.

This brief description is now enough;

To illustrate a Collective Shadow.

Other nations and different cultures

Possess their own Collective Shadows.

TERRORISM

Most people tend to behave decently;

Occasionally actions creep out evilly.

But Collective Shadows wait stealthily;

To break out to act "terroristically!"

Terrorism contrasts with civility;

Attacking people very dramatically!

Motivated by strange ideologies

Subsumed by ideas politically!

Terrorism is mostly in the Middle East

Typically, very disturbing to their peace!

Religious ideologies are motivational

Blending what is personal and social.

Terrorism is important to study;

It was a topic I taught collegially.

These were college courses in policy

But terrorists may not have a country.

Students were very motivated to study;

They tried to grasp terrorist's ideologies.

Their group reports done memorably;

As they tried to demonstrate carefully!

Terrorism demonstrates <u>The Shadow Effect!</u>[11]

Usually hidden by the "Social Collective."

However, an Evil Shadow can erupt!

Then it may burst forth like a brut!

Political ideologies do have Shadows!

Adherent may not even be aware!

These Shadows undo positions;

These are challenges to nations.

[11]   Chopra, D., Ford, D., and Williamson, M., 2010, <u>The Shadow Effect,</u> Harper & Row.

NUCLEAR WASTES

Producing weapons produces wastes!

This becomes a problem for possessors!

How might these wastes be disposed?

They last for many, many centuries!

Now this has become "everybody's problem!"[12]

How can dangerous wastes be safely stored?

Will future generations be endangered?

What disfigurements are expected?

These are important questions to ask!

Humans create pollutions that last!

Buried nuclear waste might erupt!

When might this possibly show up?

---

[12] Grossman, K., January 16, 2020, <u>Beyond Nuclear.</u>

There are obviously many uncertainties;

How long will they go on dangerously?

America buried some in New Mexico'

And locations in Nevada and Texas!

Here was one of Donald Trump's Ideas:

That radioactivity is good for you!

The term is labelled as "homesis!"

Which is a very threatening thesis!

It is apparent that leaders need to study!

Nuclear weapons and wastes are unsteady!

Future generations inherit these problems!

These have created by current humans!

CHAPTER 9: SEVEN FUNCTIONS OF ENEMIES[13]

IS OUR SHADOW A FRIEND OR ENEMY?

This is an important question to pose;

What secrets could the Shadow disclose?

What keeps us people from knowing?

Which are the features we are hiding?

In contrast, how is our Shadow an asset?

"Friend vs. Enemy?" Shall we place a bet?

These are timely questions to confront;

As this is the occasion to be blunt!

There are functions that enemies serve;

Each of these will be considered in turn.

Then readers can draw their conclusions;

By developing their informed positions!

---

[13] Middents, G., 2007, <u>BRIDGING FEAR and PEACE: From Bullying to doing Justice</u>, Manipal U. Press.

Obviously, enemies serve a media function;

A bloody fight gains considerable attention!

Audiences are fascinated by confrontations;

Ratings go up on many television stations!

"If it bleeds! It leads!" is a TV guideline;

Viewers are drawn when blood is drawn!

Victims are photographed very quickly;

Otherwise, viewers are lost instantly!

Will your Shadow try to draw blood?

Brutal assaults drawing blood and guts?

Those self-inflicted injuries and suicides----

Show Shadow and Persona collide!

RELIGIOUS FUNCTION

Religion tends to look for an evil force;

You are not surprised about this course.

"The Devil made me do it!" by comedians;

Reflecting a humorous side of religion.

Yes, "good vs. evil" is an old contrast;

But this is simplistic as a forecast!

Religion becomes more complicated;

Even religion is not that outdated!

Humans have a wide mixture of qualities;

As shown in wide ranges of theologies.

Human rebellions have dimensions;

While some religions are in one nation.

Hinduism is rooted in Old India;

Many religions are in Nigeria.

Roman Catholicism is world-wide!

Other religions are where you reside.

A few nations are seen as atheistic;

Some pseudo religion is communistic!

These try to do actions as realistic;

Others may turn out to be mystic.

Rules guide for better behaviors;

Their enemies do not get favors!

"Sins" are behaviors to be corrected;

Many rules are also then legislated!

SOCIOLOGICAL FUNCTIONS

Enemies can have sociological functions;

Thereby citizens help hold the union!

This dynamic facilitates cohesion;

When a nation tries to be a religion.

Unifying diverse people is an ideal;

If conflicts arise, this may be unreal.

When unified, much is accomplished;

As enemy-making may have helped!

The Shadow serves this function often;

Unity is essential for most nations.

Tribes are frequently cohesive;

With powerful leaders who preside.

Leaders quickly identify enemies;

This helps them wield power easily!

"Enemies" may be external or internal;

Combinations of both political and social.

The Global Earth now faces an enemy!

This is the global warming emergency!

Earthlings benefit from cohesive actions

In order to overcome fighting factions.

Many young people see this more clearly;

They see challenges for growing up healthy!

Global warming has an enemy function!

Requiring humans to overcome divisions!

ECONOMIC FUNCTIONS

Powerful dynamics occur Economically;

Personal well-being relates quickly!

Citizens preserve assets for security;

Valuing profits to live bountifully!

Traders evaluate economic partners;

Their perceived Shadows as buyers.

Profits come as results of trading;

Transactions of bold buying and selling!

If enemy dynamics do interfere

Economic outcomes will be fear;

Relationships quickly are affected;

Guilt is assessed and then blamed!

Competitors quickly are enemies;

Heightening tensions in economies!

Both friends and enemies interact;

People engaged will quickly react!

When persons engage their Shadows;

Then quick assessments will follow

Their finances will be evaluated;

Decisions affirmed or rejected!

Their Shadow has a clear influence;

To make peace or seek endurance!

These encounters become decisive;

Since Economics has a clear influence.

PSYCHOLOGICAL RELATIONS

"Shadow" is a Psychological ingredient;

More unconscious than awareness.

Living humans have many conflicts;

As the human Shadow is one aspect.

As a Psychologist, I appreciate it;

Because the Shadow is significant!

Collectively, behavior is understood

Individually comes out of the woods!

Human behavior is very intriguing;

Both physically and with learning;

As human beings, we are complex;

Growing by dealing with conflicts!

Our Shadow is an enemy and friend;

Helping to live correct and also bend!

Life is not static, but is a dynamism;

Helping each one to grow into realism!

Yes, our own Shadow is mysterious!

But we must also take it seriously!

A healthy dose of humor is helpful

So that our Shadow is respectful!

Our Shadow can be very energizing;

Contributing to our realistic growing.

Let us appreciate our own dimensions;

As our psyche deals with apprehensions!

POLITICAL SHADOWS

Politics is a very controversial subject;

People often disagree on these topics!

Democracies heighten these conflicts;

As citizens contend about politics!

Opponents "dig dirt up" to make their case!

While trying to persuade and win their base.

Naturally, opponents are seen as devious;

This makes a challenge to establish trust!

Yes, disagreeable "Shadows" do conflict;

Elections are inherently very competitive.

Opponents attack both ideas and persons;

Vulnerable participants may have wounds!

Competitive sports are excellent trainers;

Rules of games determine winner and losers!

Political players need to be in condition;

Vying to win in demanding competition!

The Shadow of participants readily show

As Shadows creep right out of their holes!

There is both sweat and blood that flows;

Winners triumph and the loser goes!

Integrated personalities are preferred;

Because struggles bring out these qualities.

Political competition uncovers Shadows;

As these contests reveals there are blows!

ARE THERE GLOBAL SHADOWS?

This is a seventh dimension to consider;

Magnifying individual's own Shadow.

This exploration is your invitation;

To investigate these huge dimensions!

Yes, our planet Earth makes Shadows;

So that our moon its own dark clouds.

Jupiter has even larger blockages;

It is the planet that is largest!

Earthlings are facing Global Warming;

Temperatures are higher due to heating.

Cloudy Shadows would be very helpful;

For us living creatures to be healthful!

Global Shadows can be metaphysical;

Consider dark aspects as metaphysical.

This lends consideration for the spiritual

Connecting individuals to the vast Global!

Metaphorically there are Universal Shadows!

Earthlings are unable to see the Eternal!

Our imaginations can also be expanded;

To imagine how Universes are extended!

Yes, we Earthlings only know partially;

Future humanity will discover more fully!

We are a small feature of the vast creation;

As researchers doing our own investigations.

CONTRIBUTIONS TO CREATIVITY

Our human unconscious is mysterious!

We fortunately shall find it curious!

Collective unconscious is our reservoir;

It helps human beings to be superior!

This reservoir is a creative resource;

Contributing as a powerful force!

It facilitates our own creativity;

Which is enriched by our mentality!

Creativity benefits from our flexibility;

To incorporate ideas from philosophy.

Deep thoughts are key contributors;

That overcome conscious inhibitors!

Flexibility opens up new thoughts;

That can get stuck in rigid ruts!

Our minds can be prided open

Beyond old boundaries that stiffen!

Our personal Shadow can open up

With new ingredients for "this stuff!"

Otherwise, we may ignore new ideas;

That stay buried by covered lids!

Yes, we may hesitate to take risks;

Because some inhibition may resist!

However, down deep, are new concepts;

Awaiting new birth by using "forceps!"

A vital key of creativity is openness;

Keep windows open for new thoughts!

The closed lid does not let ideas in;

Let life's container seek renovation!

At times our Shadow may be censured;

Reticent to add to our mind's "bowl!"

But censorship can become too rigid;

All iced up, very cold and also frigid!

Creative persons break up hard ice!

Melting it by adding sugar and spice!

Fluidity of ideas helps minds to flow

Discovering ways to warm and glow!

Originality is a prize of real value;

New inventions go into prized avenue!

Technology prospers with contributions;

Because tough problems need new solutions!

Often new plans are a target to subdue;

Ready to experiment help "break-throughs!"

A protective environment may be essential

Many concepts go through testy trials!

Most inventors go through steps for refining;

These are demanding processes for enduring!

Failure after failure tests one's endurance;

Rare "break-throughs" for top performance.

PERSISTENCE!!!

PERSISTENCE!!!

PERSISTENCE!!!

and even more

PERSISTENCE!!!

A Shadow may be seen as light weight;

But do not let that mislead one bit!

Although on a scale, it might be light

In another analogy "it is heavy weight!"

Power impact is a better measure;

How Shadows are effective varies.

Inexperienced persons may worry;

If they allow their Shadow to go array!

There is little standard management;

Colleagues may be of helpful assistance;

Therapists can guide to be healthful;

Clergy may be trained to be helpful!

Persons may develop their own insights;

They have awareness and foresight!

Reflections help their perceptiveness;

Plus greatly expand consciousness!

Balanced extroversion and introversion help;

Introverts may have greater psychic insights.

Extraverts tend to be focused on externals;

Somewhat "blind" to their own "internals!"

Introversion is characterized by quietness;

More energy engaged in being observant.

Personality development works to balance;

So that a person has maturing equilibrium.

SHADOW COMPLEXITIES

Yes, human personalities are complex;

Social interactions have a vast index.

We have social and personal Shadows;

Seen in accomplishments and gallows!

Now gallows have parallel expressions;

Hanging gallows are for criminal actions!

Artistic gallows for beautiful artistic scenes!

Plus, vast ranges between these extremes.

Shadows erupt in violent crimes;

Murder, rapes and human abuses!

Domestic killings and terrorism;

These expressions of pessimism!

Hidden Shadows are also creative;

About behaviors that are productive!

Great expressions that are superlatives;

Space accomplishments that are massive!

Humans are the epitome of creation;

Evolving rapidly into progressions!

Arts, sciences, literature, athleticism;

Moving forward into creative wisdom!

Lord Acton observed several temptations;

He clearly stated this in his aphorism:

"Power corrupts; absolute power corrupts absolutely!"[14]

Public officials may develop inflated Egos;

By not realizing their power is vicious!

Humility is a scarce quality for leaders.

Reinhold Niebuhr[15] wrote this before World War II;

"Democracy is possible because of the goodness of man;

"Democracy is necessary because of the evil in man!"

---

[14]   Acton, Lord,

[15]   Niebuhr, Reinhold, Union Theological Seminary, New York City.

CHAPTER 10: BIG FIVE PERSONALITY FACTORS[16]

Our Shadow is not readily apparent;

Human personality is not transparent;

It is much deeper than sentiment!

Yes, psychological insights have depth;

Too often this feature suffers neglect.

These are reasons to grasp onto its effect.

"The Shadow loves to play in fields of Religion"[17]

Providing persons how to handle this tension.

Religion understands with comprehension.

Human beings each exist with their soul;

Unseen to eyesight as part of the whole.

But religion grasps what is its role!

---

[16]   Digman, J., and Goldberg, L., 1985.

[17]   Williamson, M., 2010, <u>The Shadow Effect,</u> Harper Row. New York.

Humans are beyond just the physical;

As Religion cultivates the spiritual.

All persons are more than material!

Religion helps many persons to be whole;

This is also facilitated by God's own call,

Johnson[18] identified this as four dimensional.

One dimension is the "Call from God!"

This is a personal and not a fraud;

This call shows God wants your all!

A second feature is a "Secret Call!"

So personal as primarily spiritual;

A compelling reason, but mystical!

Thirdly, assess one's capabilities;

"Am I able to be equipped for duties?"

With good training to become ready!

---

[18]   Johnson, Yale Divinity School, Ct.

Fourthly, is an invitation to serve;

Matching one's talents to a position.

As a whole person for this selection

One's persona plus one's Shadow

Moderated by one's Self to manage;

All features as whole advantage!

These provide coherence to a person;

Reclaiming one's own whole self.

Authenticity become very crucial!

Psychological measures provide more insights;

These instruments are useful as measurements!

This "Big Five Personality Traits" are useful

In research, therapy and a counseling tool!

This inventory is rather easy to complete;

Typically, it can be done in thirty minutes!

Then readily understood scales are reported;

For use by professionals to be interpreted!

The Big-Five Personality Traits expresses:

"Openness" that shows inventive/curious

Vs. the contrast of consistent/cautious;

A person's who shows social readiness.

"Conscientious" is a key scale that shows:

"Efficient/organized vs. easy-going/carefree."

"Extraversion" is a third scale to interpret;

Out-going/energetic vs. solitary/reserved.

"Agreeableness" is a fourth scale:

"Friendly/compassionate vs.

Challenging/detached.

This is readily accepted.

Fifth Scale is "Neuroticism:"

Sensitive/nervous vs.

Secure/ confident.

For all Five Traits!

The Big-Five Personality Traits;

Hopefully measure into depth!

Unseen factors are elusive.

Unconscious concepts are inferred;

To counter-balance what is observed;

But not necessarily as opposite.

How can the unseen be detected?

And scientifically be measured?

These factors can be researched.

Human unconscious is conceptual;

Personality theories have suggested;

So how can the invisible be detected?

Theoretically, invisibles are inferred;

"The Shadow" has been postulated;

Helpful for behavior to be explained!

Projective measures can be helpful,

"The Inkblots" administered careful;

As persons project their internals!

Test of Thematic Apperception

Evokes human verbal ideations!

Collects a person's suggestions.

These are measured indirectly;

For interpretations professionally;

Valued by researchers helpfully.

MORE CLINICAL ASSESSMENTS

Additional assessments become available

As clinicians find data that are recordable!

Key patterns of behavior are very usable.

As clients report experience they have had!

Therapists typically develop hypotheses

That confirm neurosis and/or psychosis!

Further observations can test these ideas

That confirm or disconfirm initial thesis!

In addition, there are psychological tests;

This includes the following as available:

The Minnesota Multi-Phasic Inventory,

And the Myers-Briggs Type Indicator.

If a relational couple are involved

Relationship Inventories are used.

Unconscious material is often elusive

So "In-Depth" data are very helpful!

When Group Therapy is being employed

Interactions are helpful to then record.

Measures of Assertiveness are useful

As expressed by clients as helpful!

Co-Therapists make their observations

These can be useful for more confirmation.

Multiple sessions disclose more impressions

Compiling additional testable expressions.

THE CHINESE YEAR OF THE RAT![19]

In Chinese culture, they name years:

Then starting on January 25, 2020

This year for hope and creativity!

Chinese honor the rat in history!

According to their folk tales:

This leaping rat bit the sky!

This hole permits the sunshine

To brighten the Earth sublime!

---

[19]   Ji, Jing, January 27, 2020, "A Twist in the Tail," <u>Time Magazine.</u> New York.

"THEYISMS"[20]

Why do we often blame "them?"

Or we may abbreviate to "em!"

What about targeting "me?"

Do we humans try to externalize?

Is this pattern even politically wise?

To win games, rules reward "me!"

In impeachment trials, it is about "him!"

This is typical legalize trials of venom!

During the trial, "they become them!"

Politically, rivals criticize the other party;

Elections are enacted by contested rivalry!

News reports cover contests very critically!

---

[20]   Brooks, D., 2020, <u>The New York Times.</u>

Now let us consider contest psychologically;

Rival egos assume that they play fairly;

Contrasting uniforms of team as flashy!

But hidden are "Shadows" so invisibly

With dark agendas that are mysteries;

That are enacting with unseen tendencies.

These Shadows often have ulterior agendas;

When they take action that can frighten;

Then are "theyisms" entering a prism?

FOSTERING CREATIVITY

Creativity benefits from many ideas;

Generating new thoughts helps reveal!

So, let the eaters flow with streams

Drawing also from new dreams!

So loosen up from old constraints;

Your Shadow itself with never faint!

"Give Permission" to let them come out;

Later you can evaluate their real clout!

"Opening your windows" for new fresh air;

Can get excited that your brain is here!

Have a contest to produce the most;

Cheer yourself at different times:

Early Morning

While Eating

While Bathing

While drying

While dressing!

On walks

On steps

At stops

On roads

While thinking

When conversing

While writing

While reading

While parking.

An excellent source for new ideas:

Many occur while you have dreams!

This can be daytime and night-time

Just be ready to record any time!

Sometimes it happens unpredictably;

Let new idea flow even if it is silly!

We can ease out of our old inhibitors;

Because some may be strange "critters!"

Free up your "creative-flow-faucets,"

Let your fluids sprinkle way far out!

This helps new flowers to grow;

Your original ideas begin to flow!

Remember how you ran in the rain?

Head uncovered to wet your brain?

In rain showers you water your plants;

Then the sunlight helps ideas to dance!

Yes, creative seeds grow until "ripening;"

Sprinkle a little fertilizer for growing!

Then comes the right times for harvesting;

Ripened fruit becomes ready for tasting!

Your whole body needs nourishment;

A good meal to serve with supplements!

Your eaters will recognize your preparations;

As a reputable chef receiving congratulations!

Consumers will search for your recipes!

Your menus find customers to please!

Your creativity attracts many consumers;

And novels plus poetry gain reviewers!

Teamwork can prompt the flow of creativity;

Members may need permissions for such activity.

Teammates then feel freed-up to create;

Feeling that their input cannot wait!

Teams are quickly encouraged to relax;

Their body and mental processes can act!

Secondly, they are urged to have fun!

Even the older members then feel young.

In this atmosphere, members loosen up;

They also may get out of their slump!

Relaxed in body and mind is conducive

The team members freed to be impulsive!

Another facilitator encourages fluency;

To produce as many ideas as possibly!

This provision gets beyond old ideas;

Then members dig deeper into memories.

The fourth guideline is to engage in flow;

This lubricates their juices to let it go!

1. Relax, 2. Have fun, 3. Loosen up;

4 Generate many ideas and let it soar!

Chuckles sound out plus big smiles;

They are having fun! Not on trials.

When stale old ideas run their course

The generation of suggestions if the cause!

PRISMATISMS

The Shadow is considered "prismatic;"

Derived from two parallel dynamics.

This is the construction of a prism;

That has two reflecting "glassisms."

Prismatic persons tend to be showy;

Characteristic of the Trump Presidency.

He was very aware of his appearance;

Trying to attract more adherents!

Yes, Donald Trump lives like a prism;

Now dealing with "impeach-mentisms!"

Denial is one of his own key strategies;

By trying to deny that he is Shadowy!

His unconscious Shadow slips out;

If it is suppressed, it will pout!

But Trump had not yet managed it;

Accountants call his Shadow a debt.

This initial term of his Presidentism;

Is characterized by blaming "theyisms!"

He does contrive up derogatory titles;

Trying to give opponent bad labels!

This 2020 election year was very testy;

A series of opponents sought Presidency.

The pressure brought out dark sides;

Debates and interviews did preside!

Unpredictable developments did occur;

The Candidates did try to be secure.

They did not want to show any fear;

2020 had promised to be a big year!

Politics did develop into tribalism;

This was such a contrast to pluralism.

Tribal leaders also tried to set priorities

By reducing what were "participatories!"

Democracies benefit by wide involvements;

This pattern develops stranger governments.

Such participation does result in leadership

For more widely cultivating citizenship.

When voters became actively involved

Increased likelihood of problems solved.

Not primarily by the leader's Shadow

But by citizens' "hand on the plough!"

Trump intentionally denied reality!

He laid groundwork in 2019 early.

He claimed 2020 election to be rigged;

Anticipating he might not be elected.

"Dead people voted" got attention;

2020 seen as a "Rigged Election!"

He used wide media for supporters;

He manipulated many reporters!

CHAPTER 11: TRUMP'S NEED FOR ALLIES AND ENEMIES

Trump needed enemies whom people fear!

So that American voters will feel scared!

He selected his opponents very carefully!

So that he would be considered as bravely!

Initially, picking his enemies sounded weird!

Because he manufactured them for fear!

He wanted to be a hero for us to cheer!

A real hero who could heroically deliver!

Why had Putin not yet been chosen?

Did Trump really need this Russian?

No, the bigger that Trump could appear

He identified himself in in big league!

Putin and Trump could have gone "nuclear!"

This term could elevate their stature!

Trump said Islam was also an enemy!

Giving him marginal support of many!

WHAT WERE TRUMP'S ASSUMPTIONS?

Many insecure leaders need enemies!

They want to defend their countries!

By polarizing with the threatening

Their citizens would do their voting!

G.W. Bush contended with Iraqis!

Assuming there would be a victory!

Did he and Trump under-estimate?

Discovering Islamic power too late!

Trump's cabinet included the wealthy.

He presumed they handled U.S. economy!

Was he beholden to tackle down economics?

A false promise does not work in politics!

Trump preferred to "make a big deal!"

He assumed being the big wheel!

But government is not big business!

He was unable to control the big risks!

DID TRAGEDIES COME?

Some saw coming "Shakespearian Tragedies!"

Unfolding for both Trump and citizens blindly!

Many powerful dynamics already did exist!

Potentially crashing like an earthquake!

Who might have been a hero of a heroine?

Men can be obsessed by their wisdom!

Women are typically much more flexible!

But did Trump respect that they were able?

Trump could be rudely crude with women!

Did he assume that made him masculine?

Did his own blinders deflate these feminine?

Or did some women tend to give in to him?

Maybe Trump thought he had an empire?

Ordering people to thrive or even suffer!

World-wide, people are now wondering

Whether he failed with his own blustering!

The public knew Trump had the coronavirus;

He was hospitalized for this several days.

Now reported is that his case was worse;

He was almost place on a ventilator![21]

DID CHAOS BECOME CRISES?

Impressions for two have already come!

Trump's pronouncements were alarming!

He had declared orders so very quickly,

Both were domestically and globally!

---

[21] February 12, 2021, "Trump's Bout with Covid-19 Was More Than Officials Had Let On," The New York Times.

Immigrants from seven nations delayed!

So dubious appointments were then made!

Tweets and phone calls without consultation!

These impacted America's foreign relations!

A number of Trump's ideas were unrefined!

Examples like blunt statements included!

"High School" students would understand!

He belittled Judges who had not agreed!

Puzzling thoughts were within Trump's mind!

His spontaneous comments made demands!

His "thin skin" rebuked those disagreeable!

His staff handled remarks unmanageable!

President Trump made pronouncements

Giving impressions about his confidence!

He tended to make statements "off the cuff!"

Was Trump serious ones or were these a bluff?

WHO WERE HIS MODELS?

He may have assumed that he was unique!

Creating a new model without a blink!

But the Greeks and Romans knew tragedies

Who initially assumed their own bravery!

Caesars created their royal dynasties

Assuming heirs would then be eternally!

But this is not possible with democracies!

Nor even lasting long in autocracies!

Oriental history has had tragic rulers!

Also tried to create them eternally!

But human aspirations are misleading!

History has kept them from succeeding!

Was Trump aware of our human history?

He likely considered himself above tragedy!

Even with America power readily available!

What evidence showed he was globally capable?

GAPS

What evidence reveal to us his gaps?

His assertions showed his memory lacks!

What were his capacities to use feedback?

His staff tried to cover with alternate facts!

What was evidence of his learning curve?

Did Trump just use distractions and swerves?

Opponents already noticed his vulnerabilities!

To fake him out beyond his own abilities!

Was Trump potentially a tragic character?

Did he overcome weaknesses for disaster?

Optimistic hope could only persist just so far!

Eventually "facts" report success and failure!

His Cabinet and his staff did try nobly

Highlighting what was good over tragedy!

The media and historians both did autopsies!

Evaluating evidence and interpreting mysteries!

TRUMP'S CONSCIOUS AWARENESS

Was Trump aware of his weaknesses?

How did he cover up these surfaces?

What vulnerabilities were in his awareness?

Or were these hidden in his unconscious?

Persons may have been blind-sided!

Lacking self-insight into carelessness~

And reflections could be side-tracking;

Unaware when they were polarizing!

Actions may speak louder than words!

Cohesiveness can overwhelm swords!

And Trump could ever govern alone!

Without teamwork he would be forlorn!

Three branches must work together!

In order to have the support of voters!

Branches and agencies needed to cooperate

So that all were able then to collaborate!

TRUMP'S UNCONSCIOUS SHADOW

In-depth Psychology postulates a "Shadow,"

Considered the opposite of a conscious ego!

The Shadow expresses a person's inner evil!

A person may be unaware of his Shadow!

The Shadow persists in becoming visible!

Suddenly emptying to become hostile!

If a person's Shadow is unmanageable

Conflicts increasingly become viral!

For Trump, to manage his Shadow

This did become more debatable!

When he was confronted by opposition

Surprises came out from his disposition!

Judges did not affirm his declarations

Trump expressed needs to challenge!

He assumed he knew what was best!

He did express his style to berate!

Trump is no longer the President;

He is not now the center of attention.

He did not stay for Biden's Inauguration

He took a departure from this station.

DISABILITIES

Injuries may be hidden or obvious

Immediately visible and noticed!

Many people try to accommodate

Trying to assist before too late!

Insensitive persons lack awareness;

To most citizens this is unfairness!

"Challenged" people can be helped

And some others may be assisted!

Some disabled now feel overlooked!

In fact, they soon were excluded!

If Trump's Administration carried through

Handicapped persons did get the screw!

Trump already belittled one deformed

By a public accusation before sworn!

How were the viewers to interpret this?

Ponder seriously? Or merely dismiss?

INSENSITIVITIES

Many citizens could be left out!

Leaving assistance without clout!

Finances could become even limited!

Helpful accommodations maybe omitted!

President Trump was seen as bullying!

His clues so far were seen as shaming!

Handicapped people could be suffering!

As funds were withdrawn for support!

Did Pres. Trump have blind spots?

Blind to human problems that erupt?

His pre-occupation with television

That would cut out any wisdom!

His cabinet appointments were narrowed

To wealthy persons with high positions!

How he handled national security issues

Certainly were revealing his priorities!

Disabled persons were very vulnerable!

Dependent on who was Presidential!

Vulnerable citizens were wondering

If Trump would ever be supporting!

PAGES TURNING

Trump had been President for a month,

Both he and voters then had to-learn!

This was clearly a political experiment!

Prompting both the voters and President!

Different tactics were not being practiced,

Some cagey stepped were then being tried!

Surprises appeared daily became the norm

The rapid change prompted political alarm!

Month "two" did experience turmoil!

High heat was rising threatening to boil!

Cabinet appointments were being stalled!

Hobbling progress for legislation proposed!

Public meetings tried to unravel confusion!

Polarizations revealed serious illusions!

Media were accused of being an enemy

Misleading stories did report aplenty!

HYPERBOLISMS!

Most people wanted to feel good!

Ready to do the best that they could!

Politicians identified these as slogans!

Attracting voters to support them again!

Many hopeful voters were vulnerable!

In accepting promises as possible!

Trump had this slogan to proclaim:

"MAKE AMERICA GREAT AGAIN!"

Did readers know of Trump's other books?

Yes, we had known of one that he purported

In 2016, another book came out for review

Great Again: How to Fix Crippled America![22]

Trump also nominated a Military General

Who authored a book: The Field of Fight![23]

Indicating an aggressive military campaign!

These two books revealed their political scheme!

Trump continued to promise even more!

Using hyperboles about what to restore!

Susceptible voters continued to support

Rallying for measures Trump purported!

Hyperbolism was optimistic to the public!

"Sounds Good!" to build up this republic!

---

[22]   Trump, D., (2016) Threshold Edition.
[23]   Flynn, M. and Ledeen, M., 2016, St. Martin's Press

Trump's promises seemed too good to be true!

As they were not tested to provide proof!

LOSS OF CONFIDENCE

How could the public develop confidence?

When they received such dubious evidence?

But when the data were not very reliable,

Then different sides showed up for a trial!

What is the Dunning-Kruger Effect?[24]

It relies on evidence researchers detect!

Results discovered another contradiction

That showed up in research conclusions!

Less competent persons had more confidence!

Even without verification with clear evidence!

In fact, few incompetents will double-check

Consequently, they make dubious choices!

---

[24] Nichols, Time, "How America Lost Faith in Expertize," <u>Foreign Affairs,</u> March-April 2017. Pp. 60-73

Many of their statements were erroneous!

Announcements became spontaneous!

Incompetents may not have realized errors

They would become advocates of some terrors!

Incompetents' momentum reported to the public

Their statements did become publically idiotic!

Then they endorsed some conspiracy theories!

That then could not ever become falsified!

Their persistence did lead to idiocrasy!

These errors did threaten democracy!

This became a "Dunning-Kruger Effect!"

Which made incompetence a real threat!

One corrective measure was "meta-cognition!"

As accumulated research of false positions!

Society recovered reliance on experts!

To counter errors of incompetents!

RELEVANCE

Trump was a tragedy brewing to burst!

From peace to mishaps that were worse!

He was parallel to a bull in a China Shop!

Breaking treasures that he could not stop!

He needed to become much more cautious!

So that he did not break what is precious!

He was in danger of becoming a real tragedy

If incompetence continued as his strategy!

Eventually Congress and Supreme Court balanced!

When his Executive powers became incompetent!

America and the world had inherent resources

That drew upon competency that is generous!

Trump's Presidency started peacefully;

Soon he prevailed narcissistically.

But his term concluded violently;

His Presidency ended narcissistically.

POST-TRUTH ERA?

Were we already into a new era?

With artificial Intelligence arrival?

Others identify scientific singularity

Plus our new leadership politically!

Has "Post-Truth" politics now arrived?

Is he similar to Chávez in Venezuela?

South America had tried to survive

And Peronists in Argentina to thrive!

How was Trump's election contributed?

"Alternate Truth" has now arrived!

Media was already being attacked

Public surprises also had thrived!

Support and criticism were experienced

Demonstrators were being arrested!

The public witnessed this confusion

While some were having disillusions!

RESTORE THE DEATH PENALTY?

Trump had supported the death penalty!

By expressing his view in New York City!

Five teenagers were charged with rape!

Trump's full-page ad wanted death!

Even with another man's confession

Should have been the right correction,

Trump continued to hold them guilty

So that they would serve their penalty![25]

Was this still Trump's view of legal justice

Offering his opinions without request!

Did he support the death penalty?

Or did we need to wait and see?

---

[25] New York Daily News.

TRUMP'S DATA RESOURCES

Where did this President get his reports?

Did he have the sources that he purported?

The quality of statements that he made

In order to be accurate; not mistakes!

He repeated watching the Fox News!

Their reports did influence his views!

His biases were already well known

He reflected what Fox had shown!

"Alternate Facts" were contrived sources!

Inaccuracies were broadcast, of course!

The public audiences had been led astray

Trump tried to have it all his own way!

Did he manufacture his viewpoints?

By producing artificial news reports?

"Fact Checks" then became a necessity

In order to challenge limited accuracy!

BANNON'S TRUMP!

Appearances were significant to Trump!

Inaugurations details rather than govern!

Now he wanted to show-up very favorable

Even while he saw media hypocritically!

V.P. Pence and A.G. Sessions had ideologies

They both influenced most cabinet nominees!

But Trump lacked skills in forming policies;

Plus resentment of intelligence inquiries!

Steve Bannon's was Trump's closest ally!

He tried to roll back Dodd-Franck policies!

Did these show their own naiveties?

And readiness to cut taxes for wealthy?

Trump saw climate change as a hoax!

Supported fossil fuels like Brothers Koch!

They opposed the affordable Health Care Act

Without an alternative plan to then enact!

Fortunately, Bannon had been dismissed!

He was what Trump had clearly misjudged!

Then who had access to this President?

Family and his personal residents.

Trump loved to sign Executive Orders!

He wanted to secure the Mexican Border!

Ignorant shortsightedness was displayed!

This now shows what television relays!

CHAPTER 12: VERY ANGLO PRESIDENT!

So now we have a clear reaction!

Would this be called a retraction?

America's efforts to become inclusive

But is this nation turning too exclusive?

One minority is Secretary of Housing.

Trump avoided Hispanic or Africans!

His Executive Orders excluded Muslims!

His preferences showed for white males!

Bannon predicted fights as being relevant!

Plus advice antagonistic to government!

Trump boosted of advocating for workers!

Many rallied to become his supporters!

Then he promised to bring back many jobs!

Technologies were countering favorable odds!

People wondered about his economic thinking

This was contrary to what was also developing!

MOMENTS FOR LEARNING

Socio-economic-political new circumstances

Created new learning moments enhanced!

American voters did discover new insights!

To advocate for American human rights!

Voters' education awaited fresh starts!

For rediscovering real political smarts!

Needed active community involvements!

To exercise their citizenship for government!

Voters did need to become activated!

Advocating for changes to be debated!

Constructive outcomes were possibilities

Drawing out the best of national qualities!

Democracy expected popular activation!

In direct contrast to public abdication!

So readers, were alert for full participation

These are characteristics of voter education!

TRUMPISMS

Was Trump Making America Great Again?

What evidence would support such a trend?

Or did he try to be great, but failed badly?

Did he have vision or wondered about sadly?

Trump obviously had his own media obsessions!

He sought appearances with very large audiences!

His narcissism became apparent very readily;

His messages were shallow analyses obviously.

His other media preoccupation was twittering

Early morning tweets were likewise revealing!

Trump's messages were often disappointing

His official positions were frequently changing!

Trump avoided sharing television limelight!

He had withdrawn America from agreements.

The Global Collusion to control Global Warming

Or the Nuclear Control Treaty addressing Iran!

His United Nations address evoked laughter in 2018.

His risky positions revealed he was not enlightened!

He apparently considered relationships as a deal

Utilizing business tactics that he did not conceal!

Trump unaccustomed to a Board of Directors;

His family members were not ready as negotiators!

Moreover, his own businesses were interfused

With international affairs to be considered!

Trump displayed limited respect for women.

Indicated by his numerous affairs beforehand!

Then his own shifted on testimony given to Ford;

For approval of Kavanaugh to the Supreme Court.

In 2018, the mid-term elections were an indication

About how voters assessed the Trump Administration.

Plus the findings of the Federal Bureau of Investigation;

Along with their assessment of three years of legislation.

TRUMPETING TWEETINGS!

In order to convey his own internal ideations

He "tweeted" technological communications;

Spreading his ideas to innumerable persons

By springing his ideologies into lessons!

He relied on tersely abbreviated messages,

Assuming recipients read these passages.

These quotes required just limited logic

Trump may have assumed this to be magic!

Tweetings were considered pronouncements;

They required only minimal logical analysis!

Trump was not known as elaborative thinker

Rather as being a one-way pronouncer!

He typically wanted to be seen visually

Impeccably dressed and unique hair style!

In the winter he wore a blue topcoat!

More regal than a king in a parade!

NARCISSISM

People saw Trump as narcissistic

Self-centered, he was "Trumpakistic!"

His world views were very simplistic!

His unconscious side was Shadowistic!

Some of his actions were scandalistic.

As violations occur, he was denialistic!

His two-sidedness was dualistic

His global policies were unrealistic

He treated enemies very cruelistic!

Trump did hope to be catalistic

Many projections were probalistic!

But he broadcasted as televistic!

His efforts to become regalistic;

And his wishes to be majestic

Were failing to be fantasistic!

His blemished roles were fragelistic

His own wealth was not frugalistic

Nor were his approaches angelistic?

His comments to opponents were insultive;

His victims also found them assaultive;

This reflected a character as aggressive!

Trump's behaviors were possessive;

Some of his actions were regressive;

His tweeting became obsessive!

He gravitated as a controller

Imitating behaviors of dictators!

He tried to be the dominator!

His governing became autocratic;

Similar to Putin, Erdogan and Xi.

But Americans wanted him democratic?

OVER-EXPOSURE?

Trump often showed up on TV!

Viewers of this President got to see!

Did he love for people to view him?

Was this an over-exposer to them?

There were some risks to being seen

When did too much start to begin?

Public figures were tempting targets

For volatile and revengeful persons!

Body guards carefully followed him

Ready to protect him from assassins!

Only rare citizens may have been offended!

President Trump needed to be protected!

These vulnerabilities were always present

Particularly for someone who was President!

His schedule was often announced before

Adding to the dangers he did not face!

PRIOR EXPERIENCE

The United States is a superpower!

Some relations are positive; Some sour!

But not all nations were clearly positive

Asia had countries that were negative!

Unfavorable status had come surprises

Americans could assume all are friends!

A few Muslim nations had reservations

Plus other persons and offended nations!

Diplomatic relations could be tentative

Misunderstandings may be offensive!

Official clearly benefited from awareness

To improve relations with some success!

Ignorance is unacceptable as excuses!

Often, we are not aware of abuses!

Our President needed to be informed

Global peace hopefully to be developed!

TRUMP'S TEAM

In reviewing this poem's first 20+ pages

My earlier insights were simply "amazes!!"

O yes, specific details were unpredictable!

But his general developments were terrible!

While he continued to have voters' support

Even Republicans were dubious of sorts!

Leaders in Congress had lost confidence!

They did draw upon considerable evidence!

Trump was very naïve how government functions!

His leadership showed how he was rambunctious!

His daily tweets showed very little reflection!

He was in conflict with others who function!

Domestic issues were not very well addressed!

Leaders and Members of Congress showed unrest!

Even his own party found his leadership dismaying!

No: Major legislation had been often passing!

Senator McConnell, President of the Senate

Made statements that Republicans' regret!

Domestic Legislation was usually on hold!

Trump's leadership often did just fold!

His public appearances and also addresses

Were dismaying of the best he confessed!

His daily tweeting was not well thought out!

Prompting scatter-brain ideas that came about!

TRUMP'S HERITAGE

Discontent undergirded Trump's victories

His own negatives were overlooked quickly!

Reacted to the lethargic long experience,

Overlooked Trump's lack of conscience.

Was his victory now prompted by change?

While tolerated, he was also strange.

His obvious narcissism was a challenge,

Was his own win downloaded revenge?

His staff was trying to use alternate facts;

Were not these unusual inaccurate acts?

When facts had different accuracies;

Was this country due for catastrophes?

How can the public here and world-wide;

Determine what were facts or inaccuracies?

Manufactured data were very dubious

Hopefully to the public it was not oblivious!

Did Trump recognize racial conflicts?

A white who refused to rent to blacks?

Had he ever visited anyone in prison?

Did he know of racial discrimination?

What did he know about public education?

He went to private schools plus his children.

His Education Secretary who privatized

Did Trump know schools in crises?

Crucial items were vast military expenditures;

That did determine any offensive ventures.

Protection of American was very important

Did even Trump know what was significant?

Allies needed to know Trump's commitments:

What did "American First" take to implement?

Global crises were typically very unpredictable

But this world wanted American to be reliable!

Trump's depth of comprehension was pitiful;

His surface assessments were deplorable!

But many American failed to understand

Apparent shallowness shown by this man!

Examples included his estimates of crowds,

His inauguration witnesses were small.

But he raised questions of their estimates

His hoped for the biggest were mistakes!

Did Trump have depth into introspection?

His popular votes he called into question.

As his staff raised doubts of registration

As he does not accept tallies in election!

Initial assessments saw his superficiality

He also questioned research scientifically!

Citizens quickly noticed his lack of depth

Dependability was in the state of bereft!

What could global humanity expect?

Would foreigners be treated with respect?

Suspicions of Trump were very apparent;

By large numbers of Muslims and Mexicans!

His own cabinet had narrow perspectives;

From Attorney General to Sec. of Education.

His own advisory staff was also very limited

For assessing global issues and domestic.

Now what might our future become?

Developments were very hard to sum!

So much of the world was in turmoil;

As the future may be in quagmire!

"MAKE AMERICA GREAT AGAIN!"

Trump's campaign's own slogan!

His posturing was a big problem

His bargaining expected concessions!

TRUMP'S TAX RETURNS

For financial confidence to be gained

His tax returns can now be examined.[26]

---

26   February, 2021 Court Ruling.

His reluctance raised more suspicion

Because many people knew this tradition.

However, Trump used his choice to resist,

Suggesting he did not have to account.

While government taxes needed attention,

His own finances also needed comprehension.

Wait until he had awareness of USA budgets;

He might become aware of the nation's debts!

Full accountability to citizens would be imposed

His financial management could be exposed!

Running his real estate was very different,

Although he did know about bankruptcy!

Public finance involved over 330 million citizens

Who would tire of their President's witticism!

Trump himself had never been in the military;

How aware was he of serving on active duty?

Service personnel naturally had uncertainty

As Commander-in-Chief, would he serve reliably?

GLOBAL HUMANITY

Was Trump versed about Asia and Africa?

What did he know about South America?

Just how would he address crises globally?

Was his big ego challenged psychologically?

Did Trump be suffering from real denial?

As global warming for himself was a trial.

Facts to him apparently were relative,

As reality seemed to him subjective.

In the Middle East, Trump needed education.

He wanted America's Embassy in Jerusalem.

He was not trusted by the Palestinian crisis;

For the Israelis, he solved with high prices.

The whole Middle East is a tinder box!

Huge explosive conflicts readily erupt.

This illustrated Trump's misperception

About global issues that result in eruption!

Of course, there are diverse realities;

These always adapt to possibilities.

Personal and collective realities adapt;

To avoid falling into an old trap!

Collisions may result in many conflicts;

Ex-President Trump is falling into it.

He assumed winning the 2020 Election;

By inciting violence is not illusion.

He had taken a loyalty oath:

To support, protect and defend---

The Constitution of the United States.

But he enacted citizens to Capitol Riots.

Five human lives were then lost!

Plus property damage at a cost!

He misled his own adherents;

January 6, 2021, a sad experience!

Trump had not learned to lose!

Instead he invented what to choose.

He held a flimsy contact with reality;

As he wanted to extend his Presidency!

CHAPTER 13: INTERNATIONAL RESPONSES

Worldviews are now becoming narrower;

Trump began paying off his own supporters!

A number have very limited perspectives;

Indebted to special interest correctives.

Fears prompt very powerful emotions;

Domestic fears launch commotions.

Hatred of one's enemies and opposition;

This can prompt international tensions!

Trump's foreign policies were a problem;

He is now in power but not forgotten.

Kirshner[27] describe this very clearly;

Within just six categories quickly.

Trump was shortsighted in vision;

He was mercurial and transactional!

---

[27] Kirshner, J., March/April 2021, "Gone But Not Forgotten: Trump's Long Shadow and the End of rican Credibility, <u>FOREIGN AFFAIRS.</u>

He was boorish and profoundly illiberal;

Plus a personalist and also untrustworthy!

The Middle East is a hotbed of trouble;

Trump's views are often disreputable.

He had limited in understanding cultures;

His development had narrow experiences.

His views of Muslims were very hostile;

Precluding views of respect as mutual!

His positions of permitting immigration

Festered negative international relations!

His cozy alliance with the Israelites

Had been relished by the Jewish.

But his imbalance in arrangements

Left out the Palestinians rights.

Pretense to withdraw from the Middle East

Was resisted by American military leaders!

Arranging to assassinate an Iran General

Resulted in bombing Americans in Iraq.

Trump failed to consult before his decisions;

This resulted in wide-spread frustrations!

His own firsthand awareness was limited

His reliance of his family was narrowed!

He also frustrated European Allies;

They do not relate to his surprises!

World Affairs are also very complex

Allies do not want to be perplexed!

Trump's Russian ties were very unpredictable;

They were involved in Middle East troubles!

Did he realize Putin's goal as great power?

How do autocrats become negotiators?

Foreign Affairs[28] *collected responses from nations!*

From expert authors in international relations!

After six months, many were very dismayed!

Critically evaluating what Trump had displayed!

European nations showed great reservations!

Most were disappointed in Trump's relations!

He had isolated the USA from foreign affairs!

Leading European nations to express despair!

Germany's leader revealed many consternations!

She was disappointed in Trump's connections!

France and Italy still tried to be positive!

Russian leaders interfered with elections!

The Brexit of Britain had been unfolding!

England continued to be floundering!

These long-time Allies were very puzzled!

Hoping that America would be favorably led.

---

[28]   Foreign Affairs, Sept. 2017 issue. F

Withdrawal from North America Trade Agreement

Revealed Trump lacked value of governments!

While Trudeau, the current leader of Canadians

Diplomatically tried to continue Agreements!

Relations with Mexico were very precarious!

Trump had determined to break off relations!

His own obsession with a Big Barrier Wall!

Considered by many American the wrong call!

United States did become much more isolated!

Nations were overcoming what Trump created!

Global nations were revealing more leadership!

They did not see America in this partnership!

The unforeseen consequences of Trump:

Were more than just a gentle jump!

His unconscious pre-occupation of self

Did place America on the global shelf!

Trump did not attract experienced leadership!

He was pre-occupied with His personal self-interests?

The United States re-evaluated its own President!

Because, America had never had such precedent!

CURIOSITIES BY CLERGY ABOUT TRUMP

In early years, Trump was known as Presbyterian!

He was raised by his parents who were Christian!

One could assume he engaged in Biblical reading,

Introduced to teachings that encouraged believing!

Perhaps Trump had a Bible among his own relics!

It is unclear whether he was introduced to ethics.

Personal morals may have had some influence

How did this directly impact his own affluence?

In his later life, Trump's faith was rarely evident!

In his past life, this was not readily apparent!

Clarity was unknown about what he believed;

Perhaps religious faith was what he conceived!

Questions arose about Trump's social ethics!

Likewise, his commitment to political ethics!

His perspectives were not ever transparent;

People waited whether his views were apparent.

He occasionally mentioned: "God & Country!"

These words are typical civil terminology!

References to "God & Country" are patriotic.

These are broad but not specific to ethics!

Trump ignited anger in his divisive rallies!

Relishing television coverage appearances.

His behaviors suggested his media addiction.

Trump's belligerent language drew attention.

"Rampage" was used to describe his behaviors!

Vocal rages used to characterize his endeavors!

He tried to enthrall audiences by his ranting!

Experienced officials are much more subduing!

Understandably concerns were about his decisions!

As President, he controlled our nuclear weapons!

Citizens and officials state had reasons for worries!

As experienced officials use much more subtly!

Four Jewish leading Rabbis gave their impressions!

They were dismayed with his public expressions!

His comments about Charlottesville demonstrations

Were criticized by Rabbis for his lack of perceptions!

Americans and global citizens have many concerns!

Apprehensive whether Trump could ever learn!

The world needs leaders who they can trust!

Building better leadership is truly a "must!"

He kept referring to "Wall" of Mexicans!

Plus also insisting that they would pay for it!

This was another example of his lack of realism?

Many citizens were skeptical in both nations!!

PSYCHOLOGICAL QUESTIONS

President Trump's age was into eight decades.

This called for analyzing his personal psyche!

He was also clearly into his own later stage!

So hopefully exploration could give clarity!

It was known his childhood was protected!

His parents saw those needs were provided.

He also attended high quality schools!

He possessed basic learning tools!

His Father was successful in business.

This certainly influenced Donald's interests.

Donald graduated from Pennsylvania U.

And was engaged in a real estate career!

He entered into a field with a running start!

He had little interests in humanities and arts!

His own decisions were in purchasing hotels.

Beyond his Father, Donald bought hostels!

Donald clearly had a close career mentor!

But beyond his Father, Donald was a loner!

He assumed that he knew how to manage.

But as owner, he had his exclusive style!

Teamwork was not one of his strengths.

Rather he gave orders that go into lengths!

He did not have a Board to hold him responsible!

He had very little experience in being accountable!

At 74, questions were natural about dementia!

Did he now intentionally or naturally forget?

There were questions about Trump's own memory!

We did not have access to his reports medically!

Was this parallel to not revealing finances?

Perhaps time would show his vulnerabilities!

Questions naturally arose about his behavior!

Citizens deserved to know about if he was clever!

Dementia was mentioned in reference to Trump!

On CBS-TV 5:30 PM News, on August 23, 2017.

Voters needed to have confirmation of media!

Due to serious consequences of dementia!

More than 1000 misleading statements[29]

While serving in the role of President!

Was he forgetting? Or was he misleading?

As President, he needed to be checked!

Trump had practices of self-congratulations!

Example: "I don't believe any President has

Accomplished as much as I have in the first

Six months as I have. I really don't believe it."[30]

His self-assessments were in need of checking!

Trump had a known practice or exaggerating!

---

[29] Kristof, Nicholas, August 24, 2017, <u>New York Times,</u> editorial.
[30] Collins, Gail, August 24, 2017, <u>Washington Post,</u> editorial.

This type of self-grandiosity became dubious!

These practices influenced his conscientiousness!

Trump's mental health became a global concern!

The United States and Allies needed to discern!

Plus additional factors were likely festering!

Influenced a President's capacity for governing!

Colleagues recognized that Trump was narcissistic!

This indicated that he had thought he was magic.

He was impulsive and reckless in his "behaving;"

Plus uncontrollable in his own solitude thinking!

Trump was considered "a clear and present hazard!"

In International Affairs this was considered major!

His own impulses did result in dangerous disaster!

Nations were on alert about what could happen.

His *"Unconscious Shadow"* was then known!

He could tweet a message to become renown!

Fortunately, his Staff and Congress did manage

Those impulsive ideologies that could damage!

TRUMP'S SELF-AWARENESS

Did Trump have insight into his own psyche?

Or was his psychological functioning naive?

And did he recognize his own projections?

Was he aware of his Narcissistic functions?

He displayed lack of psychic insights,

He manipulated other with *"frights."*

"Put-downs" were frequently expressed,

As his personal ego was rarely repressed!

He saw himself as a *"wheeler-dealer"*

Winning negotiations but not a healer.

What were impressions of global leaders?

Were there current measures by raters?

American decisions are made by voters,

Competing candidates are the campaigners!

2020 was the year for major elections.

In November, voters made their decisions.

But he again tried to belittle opponents?

He tried to do this with Hillary Clinton

Did that occur with Sanders or Warren?

And with Butiego or someone unknown?

Many unknowns have been explored!

The American public was not bored.

Big campaigning did happen all over

Appealing to voters to be the deciders!

The United States had lagged behind;

By relying on just the "male kind."

Other nations have female leaders;

Electoral system counter-acted!

Due to the dated processes to elect;

We have not had a female President!

But now we have a woman as Vice-President

Even now the Electoral System is outdated!

Then Donald faced another crisis!

As the first term marker approached.

He had accomplished so very little;

Searching now for a "yod and tittle!"

Formulating policy is very complicated;

It takes much more than just to be started.

Health care policy is a very entangled issue.

Complex problems require thorough analyses!

He still tried to make up "Fake News!"

Health Care is a challenge for experts!

This is more than fixing a big headache;

Changes take almost a large earthquake!

Public Policy may be beyond "This Donald;"

He could not just make his quick comment.

He struggled, he lipped-off and badgered others;

His was faced with what was beyond his druthers!

Could Trump have generated more trust?

Beyond the people beholden to persist.

His marriages indicated more trouble;

As he tried to live in a big bubble!

He tried to retain economic controls;

Intimidating their bodies and souls!

He did have extensive global powers

Very different than hotel towers!

Power tempts leaders to extend control;

Unconscious factors erupt to be bold!

Trump did not handle needs of his ego;

Ignoring limits of what was globally legal!

DEVIOUS SHADOW

Trump's Shadow could be devious!

His actions could be mischievous.

People around him were victims;

He himself did become one of them!

How could this ever happen?

This became a very fair question.

Human Shadows are unconscious!

Consequently, they may be dangerous!

A Shadow can act out evilly!

Countering what is held ideally.

Trump did act destructively;

Breaking out even publicly!

One analyst expressed this clearly:

Not now given out for publicity.

"You cannot bring Trump down.

He can only destroy himself!"[31]

This was an analysis politically

In 2020 election year publicity.

Trump did act out maliciously

Was this done unconsciously?

Trump tended to be very reactive;

His actions were often unreflective.

These attacks created opponents,

Most were expressed at moments!

He often gave negative labels;

These did produce troubles.

This had become immature;

Showing how he was insecure!

---

[31]   Eisen, N., March 7, 2020, "It was Absolutely Worth It," <u>The New York Times.</u>

"Sleepy Joe" he gave to Biden;

"Crazy Hillary" given to Clinton.

Giving labels was so adolescent;

Not expected from a President!

CHAPTER 14: WHEELER<>DEALER

Typically, Las Vegas has the dealers,

They are associated with gamblers!

With performances of entertainers.

Commentators call these "no-brainers!"

Dealers try to attract appetizers,

Along with their drinks and dinners.

They enjoy the company of thrillers,

Along with movies attracting viewers.

A contemporary dealer is "the Trumper!"

He is also known as a "womanizer."

For difficulties, he hires his lawyers,

Who serve "troubled needing helpers!"

Out of these appetizers are emergers;

Who have scant grasp of their "Shadows!"

Psychologists are explorers even deeper;

Finding insights about all these puzzlers!

Some of the characters are deniers;

Others are election campaigners.

They all are hoping to be winners

Really trying not to be the losers!

With distractors, they need blinders,

They hope to win with the fast gallopers!

Most need to have a very good trainer;

So that they become the fast winners!

There are gamblers who are winners;

Even as many will become sad losers!

Dangers occur when gamblers are leaders;

To avoid problems, we need managers.

Traditional religions call these sinners;

Hoping that they will become "repenters!"

Some want to have more worshipers

All of them prefer "religion-goers!"

An ethical tenant is "respect for law,"

Many citizens hold the law in awe.

America has a large number of lawyers,

Verbally argumentative rather than laborers!

Trump relishes talking a big game'

But talking and doing are not the same!

Verbosity is his preference in relating;

His "tongue" was exercised while debating.

In democracies, it takes many voters,

Candidates seek votes as campaigners.

Some try to be "Wheeler-Dealers;"

Attracting attention of interviewers.

The "Trumper" was a vicious "labeler,"

"Sleepy Joe," "Terrible Hillary" caller.

He wanted opponents to be trailers;

Could his Shadow be his helper?

His negative Shadow was a doubter;

It also shouted out even louder.

He may have difficulty with controllers

By not preferring to have "monitors!"

Have you noticed Trump's smile?

It only showed up once in awhile!

How do you interpret his face?

Stern? Friendly? or an empty place?

Television exposed his excesses;

His mouth that orally expresses.

Like spewing out his words

Trying to exaggerate his terms!

When did he form his worldview?

His perspectives were often not new!

Did his public image have domination?

Still frozen in outdated information?

His own advisors did not correct him;

"Alternate Facts" were very slim.

He lived in his own contrived reality;

What was his foundation ethically?

Global audiences read him carefully;

Preparing to negotiate politically.

Trump made very quick conclusions.

How many were based upon illusions?

Could his psyche be quickly manipulated?

Was he unable to detect what is inflated?

Cross-cultural variations are different,

Non-verbal communications is a variant.

Trump gave impressions of confidence;

He prided himself with visual prominence.

He also valued "making a deal" quickly

Hoping to come out ahead financially!

Negotiating with Asians took patience;

Making it hard to know their stance.

Trump did not display patience;

This may have made him anxious.

Nuclear War results in atrocities;

It would heighten old polarities.

Did Trump have such awareness?

How to initiate global peace processes?

Did he bring enemies together?

To reduce old hostilities as negotiator?

He knew how to fire up the tensions;

How might he have managed dissensions?

Trump did not affirm global warming;

His grasp of sciences was very disappointing.

With global powers, our future is troubling;

How huge was his deficit in new learning?

His propensities to fire his opponents,

Heightened chances for tragic moments.

His was the very high-risk global leader;

Antagonizing animosities into disaster.

TRUMP'S INEPTNESS

Trump handled his roles badly;

He often failed in responsibilities!

It showed with the coronavirus;

He delayed in even warning us!

He was advised in mid-January 2020;

He delayed 6-7 weeks with advisories.

This was a failure in his responsibility

This did impair his re-electability.

Then by the end of his Presidency,

As over 535,000 Americans died!

Earlier action could have saved some,

If positive had been taken for them.

Trump displayed his own personal ineptness;

Showing he should not continue as President?

He failed in showing proper competence,

With serious limits for interdependence.

Trump was pre-occupied with appearances;

He wanted to be the center of attention!

His own immaturity in his judgment;

Showed his own incompetence.

So he became a one term President!

He had not won the citizens' confidence.

He cannot now do much more damage;

Both in the world and the United States.

Trump had become a real fright;

He thought what he does was right!

Could he see things that he did wrong?

Just when we needed someone strong!

New threats to him were a "Hoax!"

He labeled opponents as crooks!

His simplistic comments were inept;

He delayed seeing virus as a threat!

Unqualified to lead the United States;

Unable to give leadership to the world.

While Trump did then become a liability;

Not to be re-elected to the Presidency.

Other nations did not trust him;

Neither did increasing Americans.

Scientists tried to work around him;

But he did not understand them!

"The Trumper" had difficulty letting go;

He challenged the 2020 Election results!

Seven states were than investigated;

Trump's lawsuits were not enacted.

He was puzzled by the outcomes;

His close colleagues beat drums.

Factual data were also unworthy;

He imagined these ideas unbelievably!

But his legacy charges were unsupported;

Intelligence data were reluctantly shared.

His considered elections untrustworthy;

Would he be willing to face reality?

"Past President" may be unbelievable;

For Trump this seemed unconceivable.

Did he think his own role was perpetual?

Did he believe his was always Presidential?

Succession was honored by 45 Past Presidents.

But Trump saw the 2020 Election as rigged!

Was his own model that of an autocracy?

It seemed he was troubled by Democracy!

But his legal charges were unsupported;

Intelligence data were reluctantly shared.

He considered this election as untrustworthy;

Would he be willing to face the true realities?

There is often human resistance to change;

To realize we are aging is an example.

Or marriages breaking up is a trial

As denial can persist for a while.

Facing new realities is difficult;

Life changes are resisted as a result.

We prefer old comforts to persist;

Let us continue many people insist.

Who decides what is our reality?

Blaming others could be actuality!

The shifts from taking responsibility

This dynamic is seen in Psychology.

It can take time to make adjustments.

Denying reality has consequences.

Groups and persons experience this;

Adjusting to new facts has challenges.

Past Presidents have illustrated denial;

Herbert Hoover denied as President.

He denied several economic realities;

The Depression in early nineteen thirties.

Nixon's Presidency was a catastrophe!

As he handled late sixties<>early seventies.

Nixon eventually resigned his Presidency;

Vice-President then faced these realities.

Past-President Trump was clearly in denial;

Unable to acknowledge the 2020 Election!

Was he preoccupied with public perceptions?

Was he trying to show he is an exception?

TRUMP'S SECOND IMPEACHMENT TRIAL

He has faced another impeachment;

His denials were attacks on U.S. Capitol!

His radical supporters were violent

But he had denied the evidence.

Evidence revealed his incitements;

On January 6, 2021 including riots!

Trump claimed a rigged 2020 election;

He tried to show he was their selection.

But documented evidence does disagree;

The Senate held a trial in order to see.

Not since 1812 had there been an attack;

But in 2021, it was almost shacked!

Trump incited these violent attackers;

Both the Senate and House were ransacked.

He has been found to be the guilty instigator;

But the Senate does not have unbiased deciders.

While Trump repeatedly denied realities;

He could not face losing the election.

So he recruited violent supporters;

He urged them to be "ransackers!"

Evidence showed he was a denier;

Evidence to him was manufactured.

He contrived beliefs he was re-elected;

His supporters were also convinced!

Of course, Trump was again acquitted;

The Senate was not an unbiased jury.

Two-third's majority was needed

To convict him of being guilty.

He loved to assign label names;

He gave these to carry the blame.

Using these techniques that fit him;

Readers can add what occurs to them:

Here is a quote from a former White House Aid:

"The Devil is a Saint when compared with Donald Trump!"[32]

Deluded Donald!

Delusional Trump!

Dubious Donald!

Trumpy Tricks!

Trump's Cult!

Mac—Donald's!

Devious Trump!

Donald's Fries!

Donaldistic Narcisistic

[32]   CNN-TV News, February 13. 2021.

CHAPTER 15: THE ROLE OF PAST PRESIDENTS

WHO ARE THE BEST POTENTIAL LEADERS OF AMERICA?

These questions of leadership of America are very controversial.

Since the position is not inherited, elections become political.

Preferences range from a military leader to a head of a household.

Others prefer a business executive or an experienced legislator!

The United States has had historically many different Presidents,

There is only now a partial trend except all must be residents.

University Presidents and Military Generals have been in office,

Hoover was an engineer while George "w" had his own MBA!

There have been two brief family dynasties for only twelve years,

Attempts are entertained while they have never been sustained.

Governors of states inherently possess leadership qualities to note,

Bigger states have provided leadership by gaining popular vote.

We have had lawyers considered to be familiar with governance,

Earlier we had constitutional contributors with their substance.

Elected officials are sworn in to protect the U. S. Constitution,

Most have a working knowledge of what are these provisions.

While most candidates express their personal religious faith,

We have not had ministers in office, but they have been candidates

Many running for this office give attention to their own religion,

For many citizens, Judeo or Christian are their frequent tradition.

Questions prompt debates about electing a business executive,

Candidates like Romney, Forbes and Cain tout their experience.

Is leading this nation similar to heading a private business?

What are similarities and what are also major differences?

ISSUES, QUESTIONS AND UNCERTAINTIES

How is the Presidential role unique? What is optimal preparation?

In reality there is not a position even close to serving as President!

Heads of States are different from leading business organizations,

A President is primarily a public servant, not a corporate executive!

While the President is boldly called the "Commander-in-Chief,"

This misleading nomenclature gives us impressions of control!

Surprisingly, a President has very limited command authority,

But rather was a super collaborator to make decisions responsibly.

Presidents have heavy responsibilities with little control of budgets,

The House of Representatives authorized to do appropriate patrol.

Business executives have limited experience acting in public serving,

They control plans, budgets and human resources for profit seeking.

Executives in free enterprises have little experience in non-profits,

Hoover and "w 43" found they caused major depression-recessions.

Truman and Reagan developed unique styles in their leadership,

Neither had ideal preparation, but adapted to global challenges.

America does not have intentional preparation to lead this nation,

Entrepreneurial candidates decide themselves to run for election.

Most are eliminated in trial by fire in fund-raising and in debates,

This hodge-podge process sifts out the unpopular before too late!

Campaign financing demands major resources to run for office,

    The Supreme Court ruling has an insidious impact in campaigns.

PAC money may add to more corruption by wealthy contributors,

    Vested special interests will get preferential treatment trade-offs.

Citizens as voters are increasingly being educated noticeably,

    Popular media and rich donors now control disproportionately!

.

People are actually voting less as a result of these recent dollars,

    Plutocratic practices attempt to push their candidate as popular.

CHAPTER 16: NEW OCCASIONS TEACH NEW DUTIES![33]

As citizens we work jointly together;

Internal strife must now be overcome.

Coronavirus is our current challenge;

Together we will get through better.

As Americans, we do have our duties;

Our forebearers we appreciate in studies.

Biblical Truths[34] are always guidelines;

Our obligations to truth are headlines!

We value our peaceful transitions;

As we are not seeking revolutions!

Globally, we endorse best solutions;

To be transmitted to future generations.

---

[33] This Motto Guided My Address as a High School Senior.

[34] Micah 6: 6-8 and The Great Commandment.

Yes, our progeny are counting on us;

They depend that we hold their trust!

Jointly we contribute to human history;

All citizens must continue to do this duty!

When will a woman become President?

We now have a woman as Vice-President!

Women actively seek this very Office;

Increasingly voters now do notice!

Past Presidents have been helped by wives;

The Presidency has many demanding roles!

Women need to recognized as very significant!

It is timely to acknowledge how important!

A hundred years ago women be could not vote!

Americans were slow to see their own role!

Mrs. W. Wilson supported her husband;

As did previous Presidential wives!

The U.S. Presidency is very arduous!

Their contributions are notorious!

Eleanor Roosevelt is another example;

From Depression to World War II.

Post war she helped form the United Nations,

She made a number of top contributions.

Beth Truman helped Husband Harry

She stayed in his background carefully.

Eisenhower' wife was from Boone, Iowa!

Supportive during WW II and his Presidency!

Kennedy's wife, Jackie, young and beautiful!

On his assassination, she was still youthful!

Lady Byrd Johnson steadied her Lyndon;

She helped him avoid a resignation![35]

---

[35] Baker, Peter, March 20, 2021, "First Lady Coaxed Lyndon Johnson form Brink of Quitting Presidency," <u>The New York Times.</u>

The 1960's was a befuddling decade;

Lady Byrd came to Lyndon's aid.

Pat Nixon held their family together;

Through impeachment of her husband.

She had a steadying role for their daughters.

Spiro Agnew then served as Vice President.

Rosamond Carter was an anchor for Jimmy;

From Georgia farm and his time in the Navy.

Nancy Reagan was a balance for Ronald;

As a couple, the traveled internationally!

George H.W. Bush's wife was experienced;

From New England to Texas where they lived.

Then Hillary Clinton made many contributions;

She became Secretary of State for this nation.

George "w" Bush's wife grew up in West Texas;

Laura served as a balance for her husband.

Obama's wife, Michel, is very well educated

Her future roles now are still unfolded!

Melania Trump faced many challenges;

Facing uncertainties with many edges.

Jill Biden is also a professional woman;

Her future with Joe has recently begun.

Much is expected for First Ladies!

They give a great deal to our country!

While being an anchor to their family

NEW OCCASIONS FACE NEW DUTIES!

LET US EXPRESS GRATITUDE to FIRST LADIES!

BIBLIOGRAPHY

Acton, Lord, *The History of Modern Man.*

Baker, Peter, March 20, 2021, "First Lady Coaxed Lyndon Johnson form Brink of Quitting Presidency," The New York Times.

Brooks, D., January 25, 2020, *The New York Times.*

Buber., M., I-THOU.

Collins, Gail, August 24, 2017, Washington Post, editorial.

Chopra, D., 2010, The Shadow Effect, Harper & Row.

Court Ruling, Febriaru 2021, The New York Times,

Digman, J. and Goldberg, L., 1985.

Eisen, N., March 7, 2020, "It was Absolutely Worth It," The New York Times.

Foreign Affairs, September, 2017.

Freud, S., The Collected Works of Sigmund Freud,

Ford, D., 2010, The Shadow Effect, Harper and Row.

Digman, J., and Goldberg, L., 1985.

Flynn, M. and Ledeen, M., 2016, St. Martin's Press

Foreign Affairs, Sept. 2017 issue.

Goldberg, L., 1992, "The development of markers for Big-Five factor structures, <u>Psychological Assessment</u>

Grossman, K., January 16, 2020, <u>Beyond Nuclear.</u>

Ji, Jing, January 27, 2020, "A Twist in the Tail," <u>Time Magazine.</u> New York.

Johnson, Yale Divinity School, Ct.

Jung, C. <u>The Collected Works of Carl Jung,</u>

Kirshner, J., March/April 2021, "Gone But Not Forgotten: Trump's Long Shadow and the End of American

Credibility, <u>FOREIGN AFFAIRS.</u>

Kristof, Nicholas, August 24, 2017, <u>New York Times,</u> editorial.

Leonhardt, D., (March 20, 2017) <u>The New York Times.</u>

Mead, W. R. "The End of Wilsonian Era,"

Middents, G., 2007, <u>BRIDGING FEAR and PEACE: From Bullying to doing Justice, Manipal U. Press.</u>

Mortenson, G., 2009, <u>Stones into Schools,</u> Viking Press.

<u>The Holy Bible,</u> Micah 6: 6-8 and "The Great Commandment."

<u>The New York Times,</u> Feb., 12, 2021.

<u>The New York Daily News.</u>

Niebuhr, R., <u>The Nature and Destiny of Man.</u>

Nichols, Time, "How Amercia Lost Faith in Expertize," <u>Foreign Affairs,</u> March-April 2017. Pp. 60-73.

Packer, G., January-February, 2021,"The Legacy of Donald Trump," <u>The Atlantic</u>

RaVitch, Diane, 2011, <u>The Death and Life of the Great American School System,</u> Viking Press.

Schurman, J., 8/25-2017, <u>Washington ost..</u>

Thrush, G., & Habernoun, M, m (March 20, 2017, <u>New York Times.</u>

Trump, D., (2016) Threshold Edition.

Williamson, 2010, <u>The Shadow Effect,</u> Harper Row. New York.

Zubook, Shoshana, January 31, 2021, "The Knowledge Coup," <u>The New York Times.</u>

Printed in the United States
by Baker & Taylor Publisher Services